KICKING THE PEOPLE PLEASING HABIT

A 6-STEP APPROACH

JANICE ANGELA BURT

Kicking the People-Pleasing Habit: A 6-Step Approach
Published by SJ Publishing
Sacramento, CA

Copyright ©2022 Janice Angela Burt. All rights reserved.

No part of this book may be reproduced in any form or by any mechanical means, including information storage and retrieval systems without permission in writing from the publisher/author, except by a reviewer who may quote passages in a review.

All images, logos, quotes, and trademarks included in this book are subject to use according to trademark and copyright laws of the United States of America.

Library of Congress Control Number: 2022902510
Burt, Janice, Author
Kicking the People-Pleasing Habit: A 6-Step Approach
Janice Angela Burt

ISBN: 978-0-9899125-5-6
ISBN: 978-0-9899125-7-0

Self-Help / Personal Growth
Mind, Body, & Spirit / Inspiration & Personal Growth

QUANTITY PURCHASES: Schools, companies, professional groups, clubs, and other organizations may qualify for special terms when ordering quantities of this title. For information, email
janice@spanishjanice.com

All rights reserved by Janice Angela Burt and SJ Publishing
This book is printed in the United States of America.

DEDICATION

I dedicate this book to those beautiful souls who have been wounded in their past and thus strive to receive love and approval by doing and being everything that those around them would have them do and be. I know you are sensitive and empathetic, sweet and caring. Your wounds are deep and throbbing still. You simply want to be loved. You will do anything, it seems, for this love. You will put yourself down and ignore your own needs for this love. You will be hospitalized and start taking anti-anxiety meds for this love. You will give until your body breaks down and your spirit ruptures for this love. You have yet to realize that you've carried this love inside of you all along. It is there waiting to be discovered. Once you discover that you do not have to siphon this love from anyone outside of yourself, you will be free, and your life will change dramatically. You will leave your indelible mark on this world with the love that you uncover within.

I see you.

MORE BOOKS BY
JANICE ANGELA BURT

Bits & Pieces of a Broken Heart
From Broken to Open: A Heart Story

WHAT PEOPLE ARE SAYING...

"Kicking the People Pleasing Habit drew me in. This book is full of tips and encouragement that get your mental backbone in shape. Being reminded that self-care is far from selfish was just what I needed to read in that moment. Janice Burt shares her journey on going from struggling and stuck to self-love and healthy boundaries. Her raw stories are relatable, and you'll feel you've known the author for years. Grab this book, get one for a friend. Perhaps start a book club to fully explore each of the 6 steps that make this book one not to miss."

-- Lisa David Olson
Author, speaker, podcaster & business humorist

"Janice brings tremendous heart, passion, and authenticity to her work. Her brilliance has helped me and so many others shine brightly in this world."

-- Jesse Harless
Speaker, Author, Founder of Entrepreneurs in Recovery

"Janice is one of - if not the most - authentic, heart-felt and audience centric speakers I've seen. She connects with the heart of the person and the topic at hand. Janice Burt is the real deal."

-- Kevin Bracy
Motivational Entertainer & Founder of Reach One Alliance

TABLE OF CONTENTS

06 PREFACE

14 STEP 1
Choose Awareness

37 STEP 2
Identify & Heal Emotional Wounds

53 STEP 3
Cultivate and Develop Self-Love

71 STEP 4
Establish Boundaries

87 STEP 5
Decide and Do

103 STEP 6
Envision & Step into Your Highest Self

117 FINAL THOUGHTS

Preface

Preface

You're ugly.
You're unlovable.
You're a failure.
You're pathetic.
You're a loser.
You're not good enough.

Have you ever talked to yourself this way? If so, you are not alone. For years, I repeated the above statements in my head. I talked to myself as one would to their worst enemy. I operated from a place of insecurity, lack of self-love, and the underlying belief that I was not good enough. Since I didn't know how to love and validate myself, I tried desperately to get that love and validation from others. I did whatever I thought people wanted me to do and I became whomever I thought they wanted me to be. My worth hinged on whether people liked and approved of me. Because of this, I became addicted to people pleasing. I have grown a lot in this area over the last decade and it is my desire to provide some tools, resources, and hope to those who are stuck, as I once was, in a habitual people-pleasing state. In Aesop's Fables he said it perfectly when he said,

"In trying to please all, he pleased none."

If this happens to be you, don't despair! People pleasing is very common, and like with anything, you can replace some bad habits with good habits and eventually remove this nasty tendency from your life altogether.

Here are several questions to see if this book is right for you:

- Do you have a hard time saying no and setting boundaries?
- Are you consistently worried about how others perceive you?
- Do you and yourself buried under a never-ending to-do list with your own self-care constantly put on the back burner?
- Do you give and give and give and feel like you don't get much in return?
- Do you struggle with low self-confidence and poor self-esteem?
- Do you crave the approval of others at all costs?

- Do you consistently neglect your own well-being to make others happy?
- Are you drained of energy and burned out from putting others' needs above your own?
- Do you feel stuck in relationships where you give more than you get?

If you answered yes to some or most of these questions, read on!

People pleasing starts out in our childhood and stems from the relationship we had with our parents/guardians. If our parents didn't show us love or connect emotionally to us in a stable, consistent way, we worked hard to feel their love and maintain closeness to them by pleasing them, so they would be happy with us. We then carried this habit into adulthood. We became more interested in learning about who other people wanted us to be and less interested in who we wanted to be. We lived our lives pleasing others, trying hard to earn their love, hoping their approval would in turn make us feel less worthless. This might seem to work for a while, but ultimately, it becomes a dead-end, unfulfilling path that leads to burnout, frustration, and exhaustion.

But there is hope! And I have written this book just for you!

Who am I, you might be wondering, and what makes me a credible source of information and inspiration regarding this topic? I am a soul in a body, a recovering people pleaser, an inspirational speaker, a Spanish interpreter, a mom, a voiceover artist, a yoga instructor, an actress, an author, a lover of peace, and a proponent of love. My recovery journey from people pleasing to authentic power and freedom has been hard, sweet, painful, eye- opening, and ongoing. This transformation has been the BEST thing that has ever happened to me. I have been liberated from the grip of fear and the belief of worthlessness, and I want the same for you. We each have a unique calling and purpose in this life, but many things get in the way of following this calling. These include our stunted beliefs, not-good-enough feelings, fear, and emotional wounds. Often, we try to ignore these limiting beliefs and feelings, but they don't just go away on their own. It takes awareness and effort on our part to move past them.

It is my desire to break through those barriers and blocks in my own life and share my story with you, so you may feel a glimmer of hope amidst darkness and despair. I lived for many years bound by fear and struggling to be who others wanted me to be. It was suffocating, imprisoning, burdensome, and unproductive. When I was finally ready and able to see my inherent worth and deal with my emotional wounds, my life changed dramatically. I want the same for every human being who walks this earth. Living from a place of freedom changes everything.

People pleasing can be a hard habit to break. Kicking this habit will require you to look deep within yourselves and deal with your past and your pain, establish boundaries, cultivate self-love, forgive, and step into the best version of yourself.

In the following chapters, I lay out six steps to break the habit of people pleasing and become the person you are meant to be. The six steps are not necessarily linear. In other words, several of the steps can overlap and happen in varying sequences. The only step that always comes first is Awareness. After that, the steps can occur simultaneously or one before the other in any given order. It is a process, and it does take time. As you make your way through the steps, you will come face to face with uncomfortable emotions and deep-rooted pain, but I can attest to the fact that it is worth any and all pain and discomfort along the way. Have faith. Rest when you need to. But don't ever give up. Your best, most fulfilling life is waiting for you! Freedom and peace are yours for the taking.

Before we dive in, I want to share a poem I wrote at the very beginning of my journey of transformation. Read this and remember that you are not alone. Remember that you are stronger than you think. Remember who you truly are.

Wish I was feeling better, but some days you just don't.
Wish the tears would stop, but sometimes they just won't.
Wish I was completely healed, but some journeys take time.
Wish I could just jump ahead and leave this pain behind.
My heart is tarred and closed and prickly to the touch,
But someday after all the pain, it will open, oh so much!
The process can be a bitch of crazy ups and downs,
Of digging deep, of cutting in, of sobs and other sounds.
But I am not discouraged, I will keep my head up high,
For after all the cutting, I know the blood will dry.
And I have to share it all, otherwise I will be stuck
Back in that place of misery where I don't give a fuck.
Part of the process is letting go of what you think of me.
So, am I sorry that I just cussed? I'm not, I'll let it be.
The path to self-discovery is lonely, yes indeed.
But through it I believe I'll find the people that I need.
What am I to lose if I put it all out on the line?
My ego may be bruised a bit, but at this point that's fine.
Nothing to lose right now but my being and my truth.
And those two things are everything. We are all living proof.

"I lived for many years bound by fear and struggling to be what others wanted me to be. It was suffocating, imprisoning, burdensome, and unproductive. When I was finally ready and able to see my inherent worth and deal with my emotional wounds, my life changed dramatically. I want the same for every human being that walks this earth. Living from a place of freedom changes everything."

-Janice Angela Burt
www.janiceburt.com

Step 1

Choose Awareness

STEP 1
Choose Awareness

"Awareness is like the sun, when it shines on things, they are transformed." - Thich Nhat Hanh

I was sobbing in the bathtub. A voice in my head kept repeating, "You need to leave him. You need to let him go." I felt like my heart was being torn in two. He was my first love, my high school sweetheart, and my best friend. We had been married for 14 years, had two beautiful children, and I felt as though my life depended on being with him. He was my everything: my sun, my moon, my universe. I had become highly codependent in our marriage. I knew I needed to leave him due to the dysfunctionality of our relationship, but I didn't know if I could actually follow through with it. I didn't know it at the time, but this torment I felt was the beginning of awareness. I was waking up. My life up until that point had consisted of a type of sleepwalking surrounded by fear and people pleasing, which I wasn't even aware of until my marriage fell apart and I hit rock bottom.

The very first step that must be taken to break the people-pleasing habit is to be aware that you are, in fact, people pleasing. *Awareness* is simply knowing. It is being conscious of your own beliefs, motives, feelings, desires, and patterns of behavior. It is consciously knowing that there is deep pain inside of you that needs to be dealt with and that making everyone in your life happy with you won't fix it. With *awareness* you can begin to have a new perspective, one that will empower you to make the changes necessary to heal your emotional wounds, develop self-love, establish boundaries, align with your values, and ultimately, live your best life.

Tasha Eurich, an organizational psychologist and researcher, states that although most people believe they are self-aware, only about 10-15% of people actually are. That leaves roughly 90% of us walking around without seeing ourselves clearly, blind to our own idiosyncrasies.

The fact is most of us were emotionally wounded as children. We carry these wounds with us into adulthood. Then, as adults, we have this inner child within us who was wronged, damaged, and not loved correctly. This inner child of ours is rightfully upset and will not be ignored. If we become aware of this, we can work on showing love and compassion to that part of ourselves and heal the wounds caused by events in our past. We can start to give ourselves the love and attention our inner child is still craving.

This is one of the definitions for people pleasing from the trusted internet: "A people pleaser is someone who tries hard to make others happy. They will often go out of their way to please someone, even if it means taking their own valuable time or resources away from themselves. People pleasers often act the way they do because of their insecurities and lack of self-esteem."

People pleasing is rooted in fear and the belief that one must earn love to feel valued. A people pleaser is desperate for love and attention in order to feel seen, approved of, good enough. Making others happy is a way to get that love and attention. It's an exchange -- you are not giving something to that person without condition or out of the goodness of your heart. There is an expectation that you will receive approval and validation in return.

I was a people-pleasing pro. I lived my life for others, and I lost myself in the process. I went so far as to betray my own soul to please my husband. It was an unconscious coping strategy that I had begun to employ at a very early age and then took it into my marriage. At the beginning of our relationship, my husband would ask me to do a lot of things for him and I happily obliged. Deeper into our relationship, he began to demand that I do things for him. If I didn't do something he wanted, he would either get depressed, ignore me or guilt-trip me. I began to feel like I was walking around on eggshells a lot of the time and that I needed to keep the peace no matter what. I desperately wanted to make him happy at all costs. The deep betrayal of myself didn't come from these daily little things; I think I could've endured that until my dying day. No, it was during our most intimate moments together where I betrayed my soul, ignored my values, and lied to feel loved.

Our sex life had always been about fantasy. Since my husband was the only man I'd ever been with, I thought that was a normal thing. He would fantasize about other people and places and things while we were together. He did it in his head at first and then he would talk about it out loud. I didn't feel good about it, but I wanted him to feel good and be happy. I worked hard to please him. I wanted to give him everything he wanted, so that he in turn would love me and validate me. My moods depended on his moods. If he was happy, everything was good. If he was unhappy, then I had to figure out a way to make it better. I felt that his bad moods must be my fault and I was responsible for fixing them.

Four years into our marriage, he sat me down and confessed his porn addiction. Even though he had preached against it throughout our entire marriage, it turns out he was watching porn behind my back on a very, very, regular basis. I felt devastated, but the people pleaser in me didn't want to rock the boat. I hated the idea of conflict. Looking back, I wish I had been more vocal about the pain I was feeling and gone to counseling or sought outside help. I didn't know how deeply this dynamic would impact me or our marriage. Instead of facing it directly, I chose to sweep it under the rug. I swallowed my sorrow. I neglected my grief and my anger. I stuffed my emotions away. But the crazy thing about emotions and deep wounds is that they don't just go away; they get lodged and stuck in our psyche and in our bodies. They fill us with dread, panic, and disease.

A while after he confessed his porn addiction, he began talking about wanting me to watch porn with him. He said he wanted to include me in every part of his life. I fought him on it at first, as I did with a lot of things, but eventually I gave in. I felt sick to my stomach, but also intrigued while watching these beautiful people have sex. And yet, my insecurity deepened. It was a mad rush of different emotions. The next day I walked around in a fog. I felt like I had become something I didn't want to be or lost something precious that I had. I felt impure, defiled, dirty, and common.

We would watch it together, on and off, depending on how I was feeling. I felt like I was swinging from one branch to another, barely able to hold on and catch my breath. I went from "yes" to "no" in a matter of seconds. My emotions were all over the place, and it was truly not what I wanted as part of my intimate relationship. But ultimately, I ignored my inner voice. I chose to silence my intuition, my consciousness, my inner knowing. I was trapped in this fear-based, husband-pleasing, codependent prison. I didn't see a way out. I'd never thought divorce was an option for me and I loved him deeply. I knew of his wounds as well and knew that he struggled with depression and lots of negative thinking. I felt responsible for keeping him in a healthy, thriving state. I believed that it was my duty as a good wife to take care of him in the ways he wanted. So, I gave what was not in me to give, and soon after I began to resent him.

The porn led to strip clubs and then to an open marriage. One day my husband told me to "write a bucket list" of things I wanted to do or accomplish. I sat there with a blank piece of paper in front of me and couldn't think of a single thing besides being a good mom and traveling. He started to help me write it. He suggested doing something with my Spanish, such as teaching or interpreting. "Oooh, good idea," I thought! Then he reminded me that I love playing sports, so what about learning how to play tennis? "Okay, I like that one too!" Then he looked me in the eyes and asked, "What about kissing another man?" There was something about him asking me this question that infuriated me deep down. I had watched porn with him, gone to strip clubs, fantasized with him whenever he wanted -- and now he wanted me to kiss another man?!? When would he be happy? When would he be satisfied? When would it be ENOUGH?! When would *I* be enough? I was so tired. I had exhausted myself trying to please him and make him happy when it seemed he would never be content or satisfied.

Nevertheless, I smiled at him and agreed. And in that moment, I betrayed my soul. I went against my own values and beliefs. I went against what I wanted and needed. I lied to my husband by agreeing to something that was not in me to give. I also want to note that I have no judgment if you enjoy and participate in any of these activities. Everyone's life experiences and paths are different. My main point in sharing all this is to point out how we can betray ourselves. This happens when we give something that goes against our own personal morals and values, our own well-being. It becomes a problem when we give at the expense of our own mental health and happiness.

This situation with my husband forced me to become more self-aware. I started to look at these patterns in my life. How I gave and gave, but then felt resentful and unfulfilled. I started to become aware of my people-pleasing tendencies. Life has a way of waking us up. Emotional pain has a way of shaking us abruptly out of our slumber. Hopefully, if we're perceptive enough, we can choose to pay attention to what's happening before we are so harshly awakened from our sleepwalking state.

Pain is what usually wakes us up and helps us to become aware. Many times, living in denial can seem easier. I lived in denial for many years. However, denial only works for a certain amount of time. Eventually, we will have to face the truth. One way or another we will be forced to deal with the hard circumstances of our lives, and we will come face to face with what we spend most of our lives trying to avoid: emotional pain.

Do you remember from geology class how lumps of coal turn into diamonds? Time and pressure! Do you know how we as human beings evolve and become the shiniest versions of ourselves? Time and pressure! We don't become amazing, shiny, brave warriors without going through some very

Kicking the People-Pleasing Habit

hard times. Choosing awareness (which almost always involves painful emotions) allows us to take our power back to be able to consciously deal with the reality of our circumstances and our internal landscape.

I came across John Roedel's poems on Facebook. I read one and I was hooked. He has such a way with words. His poems are a beautiful medley of truth, heart, emotions, and wisdom. Here, he talks about pain and wounds as teachers and best friends:

> if we don't spend time with
> our pain
> we never learn from it
> if we don't listen to the shifting
> deep rumbles inside of us
> we will build our lives on fault lines
> if we treat our trauma like a
> racecourse to speed through
> we will keep crashing into the
> walls
> I don't believe you
> will ever "get over"
> anything terrible that
> has happens to you
> like it is a fence

instead
I believe that if
you rest with your pain
under a tree for an
hour or two
like it is your best friend
it will remind you
over and over about
how you are your most
beautiful when you refuse to give up
don't let them lie to
you when they tell
you to "move on"
from your wounds
your wounds
make the best
teachers
they have so
much to teach you
about the wealth
of courage you
have inside of you
your pain isn't
an obstacle
it's a testimony

of how remarkably
brave you are
when you want to
know peace again
after you fall
to pieces
don't speed through
your recovery
lie down with your
fat tears on
the couch
for as long as
it takes
to remember
there is absolutely nothing

that can stop you
you don't need
to overcome anything
like it is a wall
you just need to rest
for a bit
and that's how you

come back to yourself again
one long nap at a time
my love,
take your time
to heal

Healing takes time. Learn to be patient with the process. After my divorce, I slowly began to become aware of all the pain inside of me that I had buried. I also became aware that I didn't really know what I liked or disliked, who I was, or who I wanted to be. I felt like a shell of a person. It was hard for me to say "no" to people (especially those closest to me). I loved making people happy and in order to do that, I became what they wanted me to be. I got really good at wearing different masks and pretending to be someone I was not. I started realizing that I needed people to affirm me and validate me to feel like I was good enough. Whenever I felt someone's disapproval, I would despair and try to figure out how to make it right. I was constantly second-guessing myself. This level of awareness was the beginning of a huge transformation in my life. I don't know that I would have given myself this label back then, but now I know it to be certain: I was addicted to people pleasing.

Every single change in our life is the result of awareness. We can't change something we don't even know exists. If we believe our people pleasing is simply being "nice," then we haven't reached the deepest level of awareness yet. Eventually, life has a way of making us aware of certain things that we refuse to see. For me, it took doing things that were against my values and moral code to become aware that I was addicted to people pleasing. The pain that I experienced as a result of my people pleasing became unbearable.

Well-known author, teacher and coach Tony Robbins says,

"Change happens when the pain of staying the same is greater than the pain of change."

The pain of staying in my dysfunctional relationship became greater than the pain of leaving my marriage, and I eventually chose the pain of divorce and the unknown. My hope is that by reading this book, you won't have to experience so much pain before deciding to move away from any people-pleasing tendencies that may exist within you.

The line between people pleasing and being a genuinely kind and loving person can definitely feel blurry if we don't actively work on self- awareness. I used to think that I was truly a nice and kind person. And sometimes I was. But other times, deep down, I was playing a role and pretending to be someone I was not so that I could feel loved, or I was being disingenuous to keep the peace. The main distinction is intention. *Why* are you doing what you're doing? Are you trying to get someone to like you, to compliment you? Are you trying to avoid conflict at all costs? What if you go out of your way for someone and you don't get acknowledged for it? Will it cause you to be resentful and hold a grudge? These are some great questions to ask yourself if you're unclear about your intentions.

If we've been people pleasing for long enough, we may have cultivated an inner sense of self-righteousness. We might think we're kind and generous and giving. Look everyone at how great we are! We don't even realize we're doing these things to GET something for ourselves. If we're aware enough, we can start to see that our people pleasing is actually selfish. Had you told me this when I was knee-deep in my people-pleasing behavior, I would have been downright offended. I would've justified my actions and expressed how I really was a kind and noble person, putting others above myself, and making myself the sacrificial victim and martyr. It's hard to see our own bullshit sometimes.

Let's say your friend has asked you to help her move over the weekend. If you genuinely want to help your friend because you value the relationship and she means the world to you, then that's perfect! You are being kind and helpful out of the goodness of your heart and the gratitude you have for the friendship. If, however, you want her to be indebted to you, or you expect her to treat you to dinner and drinks afterward, or you want her verbal validation and you know that you would become resentful if one or all of these things didn't happen, then your intentions are probably less than pure. Whenever we try to control how another person perceives us or thinks about us, we are manipulating them. We unintentionally manipulate others to make ourselves feel better.

I felt a strong need to be liked and approved of. That need came from a wound. As a child, I often felt emotionally neglected and developed a belief that I needed to prove my worthiness and lovability by making others happy. I needed to heal that wound before being able to see the difference between true kindness and people pleasing. Being a kind and generous person is legitimately awesome! To be able to give without expectation—because you have a solid sense of self built up—is amazing. At that point, you don't need anything in return. This takes time, and if you're not there yet, it's totally okay! You will get there. It just means you need to spend more time working on yourself. You need to heal more and grow more. You need to develop more self-confidence and self-love. We will dive deeper into how to heal emotional wounds and develop self-love in the following chapters, but the key is to shift your focus on developing and growing yourself (physically, mentally, and spiritually) instead of focusing on getting your needs met by other people.

Ultimately, people pleasing serves as a distraction from our own pain. Instead of taking the time and effort to heal our deep, emotional wounds, we deflect away from ourselves and latch onto others. We get what we are looking for from them instead of doing the work to get it from ourselves. Instead of validating and loving ourselves, we search for those things from others, many times at a huge expense to our own well-being. This could look like taking a job just because you think it will make your partner happy or going to college to make your parents happy even though you know you are an entrepreneur at heart and want to build your own business. It can look like doing a million favors for other people while you let your own projects fall to the wayside. It could look like agreeing to doing something that goes against your own moral values just to feel loved and accepted.

At the end of the day, when we agree to something just for the sake of avoiding confrontation or in order to make someone else happy at the expense of our own overall wellness, we are guilty of misleading the other person. We are unintentionally lying. Sometimes, if we lack the awareness, we can even be misleading ourselves. We tell ourselves we're doing it because we are such a nice person, or we just want to see others be happy, without realizing our falsehood and how much we've become a ghost of a person. But, ultimately, we're wearing a mask. We're pretending to be someone we're not. We're overextending ourselves just to feel accepted and good enough. We are trying to fill a void.

To eradicate these people-pleasing tendencies, we must first understand where they come from and identify the root of the problem (our core wounds). I deeply believe in getting way down to the root and starting there instead of just covering up the symptoms. It's exactly the same as a physical wound. If we cut our knee, we have to clean it out and disinfect it before bandaging it up.

The cleaning process involves some pain, burning and discomfort. However, it's totally worth the pain because cleaning the wound allows for it to heal properly. If we don't clean and disinfect the wound, it could get infected and our symptoms will worsen. It could even result in amputation or death. The same thing happens with our emotional wounds. If we don't examine them and do the hard work of shifting our perspective and choosing to forgive, the emotional wound will get worse and worse, resulting in mental and emotional disorders and distortions.

Many people don't want to do this work because their core wound tends to take them back to their childhoods and how they were treated by their parents or guardians. If we have experienced abandonment, rejection, or abuse, a very deep fear haunts us in our adult life. It feels awful to be left behind or neglected, no matter the reason. Children don't know how to process the actual situation, but they do know how it makes them feel. Many children from divorced homes feel it's their fault and that they did something to cause their parents to split up. If a child has been abused, many times they can feel as though they deserved or caused the abuse. These feelings, as unfounded as they are, translate as truth in the child's brain.

It is our job, as adults, to heal from the emotional wounds inflicted on us in our youth. It requires courage and determination. It's not easy looking back at something that was scarring and trauma-inducing. It is painful. Sometimes you might feel like you'll drown if you do. But I am here to tell you that you will get through it. Many times, seeking professional help from a counselor or therapist is necessary to navigate this process, especially if there was deep trauma or abuse in your past. No matter how you choose to do it, healing your emotional wounds will allow you to live your best life, to be fully yourself, and to impact those around you positively. This is all part of taking personal responsibility for your life. It is hard, but I can't emphasize enough how much it's worth it! Instead of blaming and being stuck in victim mentality, you are choosing to become empowered.

As I examined my pleasing behaviors, I started to see there was more beneath the surface. I started looking at my past and realized the root cause went way back—and it needed to be addressed. It had to do with feeling emotionally neglected and abandoned. Those were hard feelings to contend with and there definitely were times in my healing process when I felt like the process of personal growth and introspection was just too much. I would feel completely overwhelmed, destroyed, and broken. When those moments arose, I simply backed off a little bit, took a break from the emotional introspection, and gave myself permission to be in a place of grief and heartache. I would cry and scream and write sad poetry. And then, after a couple of days, I would determine that I was strong enough to give it a go again, get back in the ring and keep fighting. Changing lifelong patterns of behavior takes time, practice, and diligence. It's a bit like Rocky Balboa training for his championship boxing match. However, no matter how much time and effort it takes, liberation is always worth fighting for. The beauty and peace on the other side is indescribable. You will feel a million times lighter and a thousand times happier. You will trust yourself and feel proud of yourself. You will love yourself and value yourself like no one else can. You will be living YOUR authentic life; the one meant just for you and no one else.

Another thing to note is that kicking the people-pleasing habit is a process, as is healing emotional wounds. It doesn't happen overnight. Know that it is a journey of going deeper and gaining more wisdom. View it as an onion with many layers. You peel back one layer, and it makes you cry. Then you heal that part of yourself and peel back the next layer, and you cry a little more.

Be willing to accept this process and even be grateful for the journey of awareness and healing. Be grateful because not everyone chooses this narrow path. Many choose to hang on to their addictions, their grief, their anger, their unconsciousness. They choose to stay in victim mentality because it feels better to blame someone else than to take responsibility for their own thoughts and actions. This is not the path for you, my friend. You are choosing awareness with brave eyes wide open. You are choosing to take control of your life by examining and healing your past so that you can live a full, amazing, joyful, vibrant life. It is well worth the work and the discomfort.

To help you become aware, set aside time for deep reflection. Ask yourself questions about your views, your thoughts, your beliefs. Explore them like you would an old cave searching for treasure inside. Sometimes we might find some things within us that no longer serve us or are holding us back. At this point in the process, it's enough to simply be aware and notice. You don't need to change anything or feel shameful or guilty about what you find deep within. This is a time to get curious and observe. Write down what you discover about yourself. So many times we run on autopilot. We go through the motions in life, but rarely take the time to sit down to ponder and reflect on our thoughts and behavior. It is imperative that we take the time to get to know ourselves.

Another great tool for gaining more awareness is to develop a meditation practice. We have so much wisdom within us, yet we tend to speed through our day-to-day lives without allowing the time and space to access it. Give yourself the gift of silence and stillness. As you gain awareness of any people-pleasing tendencies you have, you can start to explore why you have these tendencies. As you explore why you have these tendencies, you can then start to heal the wounds and eradicate the root of the problem. A good starting point is to simply pay attention, notice, observe.

I pay attention to the ache. I feel it deep inside.
I pay attention to the fear, telling me to run and hide.
I pay attention to the trigger, each time you pull it back.
I pay attention to the feeling. It feels a bit like lack.
I pay attention, so I can grow. I want to shine so bright.
I pay attention, so I can change. I am here to be a light.

Step #1:
Choose Awareness

STEP 2

Identify & Heal
Emotional Wounds

Step 2
Identify & Heal Emotional Wounds

When I was five years old, my parents left on a three-week trip to Alaska. They took my brother with them and left me behind. I don't have very many memories from when I was little, but I distinctly remember pacing back and forth in my grandma's room (she was in charge of watching me, along with her four foster kids), crying my eyes out missing my family so much. I thought they had left me and that I had done something horrible to deserve it. Maybe just *me* being *me* caused them to leave? I couldn't remember what I had actually done that was so bad as to warrant abandonment. The only conclusion my young mind could come to was that I must have been unlovable.

Children have a tendency to internalize everything and think things are somehow their fault. At five years old, I took this "abandonment" very seriously. I remember sitting down and writing them a letter, as best I could with my limited writing skills at that age, telling them I missed them and asking them to please come home. I have a picture of mom and me hugging in the airport when they came home. Tears streaming down my face, clinging to her for dear life. In that moment, I must have subconsciously made a vow to never do anything that would warrant being left behind again. I began pleasing others so that they wouldn't leave, and I would feel safe.

We all have emotional wounds, and they are deep and painful and sometimes even hidden from our own consciousness. Many of us have experienced emotional trauma. The Jed Foundation describes trauma, saying, "A traumatic event can be a single event, a series of events, or a set of circumstances that we experience as physically or emotionally harmful or disturbing. They can happen suddenly, like an accident or assault, or they can evolve slowly over time, such as the toll taken by long-standing abuse or neglect." Emotional wounds and trauma can look like abuse (verbal, physical, sexual), neglect, abandonment, death of a loved one, bullying, or inconsistent, unstable love by our parents, just to name a few.

While doing research for this book, I talked to many people who struggle with people pleasing.

Each of them had some deep emotional wounds from their past they say attributed to their need to please others. One woman remembers being kicked in the stomach by her father and sent to her room during a party. Another woman recounts how she became the "mom" when she was eight years old because her parents were always absent and neglectful. She remembers the verbal abuse vividly as her parents told her she was worthless. Still another talked to me about the years and years of sexual abuse by one of her family members.

Many times, people pleasers begin pleasing others as a survival tool. If you receive a beating every time you talk back to your parents, you are going to stop speaking out so as to not get hit. Your brain will people please as a means to keep you safe and protected. It becomes a coping mechanism. It serves a purpose when we are young, but it is up to us to learn, as adults, how to rewire our brains, so that it stops defaulting to pleasing others as a means of protection. One of the best things we can do for our personal growth is to identify and heal these wounds.

I want to note that dealing with deep trauma is outside of the scope of this book. I am not a licensed mental health practitioner. If you have experienced trauma in your past, I **highly suggest getting psychological help. There is no easy way around it. Trauma has to be dealt with so that it doesn't ruin your life and relationships. If you know you have deep trauma holding you back in life, make it a priority to address those issues. You are brave and strong. You deserve a life of freedom and joy. In order to access this life, you must first address the trauma.**

To identify emotional wounds that you may be blind to, notice the difficulties you tend to have in life, specifically in relationships. In doing so, you will recognize patterns. Those patterns usually reflect what you endured in childhood. For me, I started noticing a lack of trust in my relationships and a deep feeling of not being good enough. I feared abandonment and rejection, and I struggled with jealousy and insecurity. I can look back at my past and identify exactly where I first experienced those feelings.

Emotional wounds can create triggers. When we experience something that reminds us of or feels too familiar to a painful past experience, we can step into "fight or flight" mode. We jump right back into survival instinct. To heal from these emotional wounds and triggers takes time and effort, but it can be done! One of my triggers is seeing when men give beautiful women their attention. When a beautiful, feminine woman walks in the room, I instantly feel insecure and not good enough, and this feeling is heightened when I see men acknowledge her beauty. I have seen this become a pattern in my life and in my relationships with men.

I used to criticize and beat myself up about it (which only made me feel worse), but now I recognize that these feelings are the result of emotional wounds from when I was in high school. I've examined my past and I know exactly when it started. When I was a teenager, I buried my desire to feel admired and desired by boys. I dressed as a tomboy and acted as "one of the guys" even though deep down I wanted to be seen and admired as a beautiful girl. I did this because I was scared of sexuality.

One day when I was 16 years old, my parents told my brother and me they wanted to meet us at Carl's Jr. to talk about something. As we were all eating our hamburgers, my dad said, "We brought you here to tell you that I struggle with homosexuality, and we don't want you to hear it from anyone else first."

What?!?

I didn't see that coming, especially since we were heavily involved in the church and my parents had been missionaries in Mexico City for five years. Homosexuality wasn't exactly accepted in those circles. My mind was so confused, and I didn't know how to process that information. It was overwhelming and scary. So scary. My dad was not who he said he was. He'd been lying to me my entire life.

My parents assured us that they were going to counseling and he was going to work through it. They assured us they were still together. Everything was fine, they said. But it wasn't. In my head, it truly wasn't. It was beyond what I could wrap my mind around. If my dad, who was my idol, wasn't who he said he was, then nothing was as it seemed. Nothing could be trusted. I pushed this information to the back of my mind and continued with my life as though nothing had happened. However, my inner world shifted that day. Knowing this about my dad caused me to feel like sex, sexuality, and sexual attraction were bad, scary, and uncertain. They had to be hidden and lied about and always came with a trace of betrayal.

Given my dad's homosexuality and double life, along with the church's influence regarding sexuality, I decided that it would be easier if I made myself less attractive by being a tomboy. So, I dressed in baggy clothes, wore no makeup, played sports, and joked around with all the guys, wishing I could be one of them. Boys seemed to have it easy. There was no drama, no cattiness, no jealousy. Friendships with them felt easy and carefree. However, I repressed a very feminine side of myself. The side that wanted to be beautiful, seen, and admired. I would feel immense jealousy when my friends who were girls would get boys' attention. I secretly craved that type of attention, but it also scared me. So, I hid behind a mask. I felt jealous and unhappy, but at least it was safe there.

As I dug deep into my past and started recognizing how certain events shaped my perspective and thoughts, I've been able to identify the root cause for my triggers. This knowledge has given me more power to replace negative thoughts with empowering ones and to work on my cognitive distortions (thought patterns that cause people to view reality in inaccurate—usually negative—ways). Can you identify the root cause of some of your triggers and people-pleasing behaviors? It is important to acknowledge and be aware of where these coping mechanisms stem from to be able to heal.

Digging into my past has also allowed me to have compassion for myself. I can view myself as a little girl whose parents left her for a long period of time without her knowing why, or as a teenager who desperately wanted something that also terrified her. I then can feel empathy and compassion for the adult version of myself who still has those thoughts and feelings lodged somewhere in her psyche.

I would encourage you to also have compassion on the parts of yourself that are still wounded. Instead of putting yourself down for having certain patterns, tendencies, triggers, or reactions, try sending even more love to the child inside of you who is hurting. Compassion and love heal us. Judgment and criticism harden us. You must be very intentional in viewing yourself with compassion and love. It won't just happen on its own. If left to your default, you will lean toward criticizing yourself and negative thinking. You will need to *intentionally* view yourself in a different way.

Shortly after my divorce, I went to a hypnotherapy session. I didn't know anything about this mode of therapy, but I was desperate for relief from my inner pain and turmoil and vowed to try all the therapies and techniques I could find. I was searching for relief and a solution to my emotional pain. During hypnotherapy, the therapist guides you into a theta brain state, so that you are deeply relaxed, and then asks questions. Your answers come from this unique mental state, giving you access to your subconscious, bringing up things that you may have buried or stuffed deep down.

Hypnotherapy ended up being highly transformative for me.

During my first session, I was able to see all the fear I had inside of me. At that moment, I realized that I had been living from a place of complete fear. I was able to release that fear (in my mind's eye) and create an empty space within me, one that I could fill with love. During subsequent sessions, I was able to see the highest version of myself and feel total and complete peace. When asked to envision the highest version of myself, I pictured a woman in a white, flowing dress on a cliff overlooking the ocean. She was standing tall, heart forward and shoulders back. She felt confident, powerful, peaceful, and full of love. I knew that I was that woman. I also knew, in that moment, that I would now be able to step into that vision and actually *become* that woman. She was *me* underneath all the fear and pain and insecurities. She was the real, true, authentic me.

Often, we hold onto wounds, pain, and anger in our subconscious, and we're not even aware that those emotions and blocks are there. Our subconscious also holds many false and limiting beliefs. I highly recommend working with someone who can help guide you to the root cause of the pain and begin to resolve those issues instead of only focusing on the symptoms. This is a process that takes time and effort. Have patience when exploring your subconscious. Many times we bury painful past events in our subconscious so that we can function in life. The uncovering of these traumas takes time, commitment, energy, and effort.

Once you've identified your wounds, triggers, and root cause, you can work on healing them. *You can't heal what you don't reveal.* You must take the blinders off to see the work that needs to be done to resolve and heal those wounds. Unexpressed wounds and emotions never die or disappear, they simply get buried alive and come back in the form of a monster.

I was running by the river one day. It was about six months after my divorce. I had been struggling so much. I'd been feeling so much anger, resentment, sadness, and pain. As I ran, I began to cry and allow myself to feel all my emotions. Ever since that day in Carl's Jr. when my dad revealed that he had been living a double life, I became good at repressing my emotions. They were all lodged inside of me in a massive, twisted ball of heaviness and hurt. As I ran and cried, I realized that I needed to release this hurt in some way. I needed to let go and surrender. Intuitively, I knew I needed to forgive. I forgave myself first that day on the river, and then as the days passed, I was able to forgive those in my life who had knowingly or unknowingly caused me pain.

Forgiveness is the first and primary step in healing our emotional wounds. Forgiveness is for you, not the people who have harmed you. Forgiveness entails releasing anger and bitterness and feelings of ill will. It does not mean that you need to have a relationship with that person (except if you're forgiving yourself, then I obviously would encourage you to keep that relationship 😊), and it does not mean you are excusing or condoning their behavior. It simply allows you to clear your heart of the heaviness of anger and resentment, so that you can be free to live the life you were always meant to live.

There are some amazing, mind-blowing stories about forgiveness. I remember reading about Scarlett Lewis, whose son, Jesse, was shot and killed during the Sandy Hook Elementary School shooting, the biggest shooting in U.S. history at that time. She was obviously devastated and filled with rage. She said that her anger sapped her strength and energy. Eventually, she made the choice to forgive. She said,

"Forgiveness felt like I was given a big pair of scissors to cut the tie and regain my personal

> *power. It started with a choice and then became a process with no neat ending."*

Forgiveness is powerful. We owe it to ourselves and our most magnificent future to make the choice to forgive.

Interestingly enough, forgiveness also allows us to be more creative, have a more relaxed mind, and develop better problem-solving abilities. In Vishen Lakhiani's book, "The Code of the Extraordinary Mind," he describes paying thousands of dollars to attend a program aimed at improving his thinking and creativity skills, as well as helping diminish his stress and anxiety. He was hooked up to a machine that recorded his brain waves. As he worked through mental activities, he could see the results of what was actually going on in his brain. The goal was to increase alpha waves, which are associated with high creativity, insight, compassion, and love. The secret to increasing alpha waves turned out to be just one thing: Forgiveness. He had to work on forgiving every single person in his life who had wronged him, even for the smallest infractions. His alpha waves spiked every time he forgave someone. Forgiveness is the singular most powerful tool we have at our disposal to heal our wounds and be set free.

Another way to heal our emotional wounds is to give them a new meaning. If we constantly feel like we are damaged goods or give our experiences negative and disempowering meanings, we can get trapped in feeling sad, angry, or vengeful. There is a season to grieve and allow ourselves to feel these emotions. In fact, I strongly suggest feeling all the feelings. Otherwise, they get stuck in our minds and bodies. The problem is not with feeling them; the problem is when we don't acknowledge them or when we cling to them for dear life and refuse to let them go. The stages of grief exist for a reason. We need to go through all the stages, being careful to not get stuck halfway through. The five stages of grief outlined by Elisabeth Kubler-Ross are denial, anger, bargaining, depression, and ultimately acceptance.

The meaning we give to our pain can become our purpose. One of the best examples of this is the mom, Candy Lightner, who lost her 13-year-old daughter to a drunk driving accident and created the non-profit organization, M.A.D.D. (Mothers Against Drunk Driving). Candy took this negative, horrible event and turned it into her life's mission. Her organization has helped spread the message of the importance of not driving while intoxicated. She gave her tragedy a new meaning. It was still a tragedy, but she used her anger and sadness as fuel to create a new, empowering story and make a difference in the world. Her purpose was born out of the death of her daughter.

I have a friend who endured years of sexual abuse as a child. She now chooses to view everything that happened to her in the past as a gift. Every situation and circumstance have contributed to her being the person she is today. She acknowledges that without the abuse, she would not have the depth of strength, strong character, and ability to help others that she has today. What an amazingly liberating shift of perspective! This type of perspective didn't happen for her overnight. It took years of suffering and shame for her to finally CHOOSE to view the abuse she endured as a gift. That choice has changed her entire existence and the way she shows up in the world. **The past only exists in our mind, and we have the amazing ability to give it a new, empowering meaning.** Forgiveness and giving our pain a new meaning are powerful tools we can use to heal our emotional wounds.

Using these tools, along with psychological help, if need be, can truly make all the difference in healing emotional wounds and kicking the people-pleasing habit. Other tools to help in the process of healing emotional wounds are practicing breathwork, doing yoga or some type of movement regularly, sticking to a routine, being outside in nature, practicing a mentality of gratitude (trading expectation for appreciation), doing things that bring you joy, and being creative just for the sake of creating.

"Character cannot be developed in ease and quiet. Only through experience of trial and suffering can the soul be strengthened, ambition inspired, and success achieved." – Helen Keller

Step #2:
Identify & Heal Emotional Wounds

STEP 3

Cultivate and Develop Self-love

Step 3
Cultivate and Develop Self-love

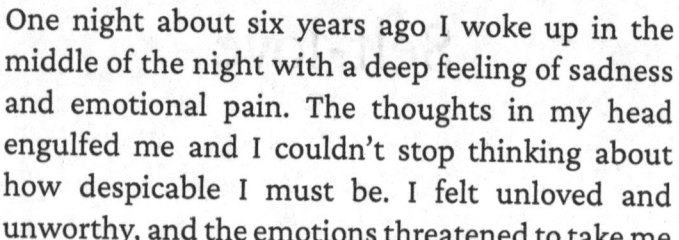

One night about six years ago I woke up in the middle of the night with a deep feeling of sadness and emotional pain. The thoughts in my head engulfed me and I couldn't stop thinking about how despicable I must be. I felt unloved and unworthy, and the emotions threatened to take me under. I sat down, and accompanied by my tears, I wrote this:

> "The night stretches on, beyond inftnity, it goes on and on.
>
> I wrestle with my demons. They are suffocating me once again.
>
> Clawing at my soul. Causing me to question my sanity.
>
> The demons feel Larger than Life and they pin me down.

Finally, something inside of me shifts and I am able to wiggle free.

As I do, the tears come violently. As if being trapped inside for a lifetime.

I open my mouth and scream, but no sound comes out.

I scream silence again and again.

I get up and go to the bathroom. I turn on the light and look at myself in the mirror.

'You are hideous,' I tell myself. 'I hate you so much,' I whisper through the tears.

As I say this, I feel the demons retreating. Even they are not interested in me anymore."

Self-hate is a real thing. I've experienced these feelings of deep contempt for myself. I've also experienced the opposite. I've experienced a profound love for myself that made me weep with happiness. I always strive to return to that love.

In Eckhart Tolle's book, "The Power of Now", he recounts a parable about a beggar woman who came out every day to beg for money. She would sit at the same street corner on the same crate- like box, day in and day out. Some people would stop and throw some coins into her lap. Others would barely glance over and her and briskly keep on walking by. One day a gentleman passed by and asked her what was in the box she was sitting on.

She told him she didn't know, but he insisted on knowing. She was irritated because she was fairly certain there was nothing of value in the box, but got up and broke it open, just so he would go away. She was astonished when hundreds of gold coins spilled onto the ground. She'd been sitting on treasure for years and never even knew it!

We each have the most amazing treasure within us. This treasure is Love. We search to get that love from people around us, but ultimately what they give us are scraps compared to the deep love we carry within ourselves. It is our job to uncover this love-- to split the box open and enjoy this priceless treasure. Instead of trying to get that love from others, we can focus on getting it from the Source itself.

To rid ourselves of the people-pleasing habit, we must not only develop a solid sense of self, but a complete love for ourselves as well. If we don't, we will constantly be searching for that love outside ourselves. We will look for it in strangers and family and lovers and children. We will search high and low for this love. We need to realize that the love we long for is inside of us and has been there all along. We just need eyes to see and the awareness to know that it is available to us whenever we need. I wrote the following poem one night as I was working on developing my own self-love:

I live in a world of movement. Circles and cycles of insanity.
I stand amidst the chaos choosing who it is I want to be.
We have to dig deep, my warrior friends, to find our worth within.
It won't come from there or this or that, and it certainly won't come from men.
We need to stop consuming lies and recognize exactly what they are.
Illusions. Half-truths. Deception. Distorted perception. It's time to raise the bar.
Judgment. Condemnation. Rejection. Unworthiness. I refuse all these.
Give me instead wholeness, acceptance, love, unity, and peace, please.
Fellow women, stand up tall and join me on life's stage.
Strong and confident. Beautiful and righteous. We're all on the same page.
Refuse the lies. Dig deep and breathe. Remember to be brave.
Be kind to all. Believe your worth and climb out of your cave.

Self-love is the ability to love, honor, and value yourself. It has nothing to do with how others perceive you and everything to do with how you view and treat yourself. In order to truly love others, you must learn to love yourself first. Self-love is not to be mistaken with arrogance or looking to get your needs met at the expense of others. Self-love is having a deep appreciation for oneself. It is knowing that you are valuable, lovable, and worthy. It is accessing this love within yourself so that you are not dependent on getting it from others.

When you people please, it may appear that you are loving others, but the intention is not to *give* love, it's to GET love. It's like a slight-of-hand in magic. It's not really what it seems. It turns out that people pleasing is actually manipulation and deception, which don't equate to love at all. The craziest part is that most times it's completely unintentional! We don't even know we're doing it.

I have a friend who does everything for everybody but feels depleted and lacking energy most of the time. In her romantic relationships, she has always bent over backwards to make sure her partner has all of his needs met, yet her needs go unmet. She doesn't even allow her partner to meet her needs because she won't communicate them out loud. She gives and does everything for her partner and then ends up resenting him. The problem is she doesn't love herself enough to show him the real her, imperfections and all, and she hinges her worth upon his approval and validation. She has just begun to realize this pattern in herself and is doing the hard work of changing. It's painful to recognize and acknowledge these parts of ourselves, but the sooner we do, the sooner we can make the necessary mindset shifts to transform our lives.

I was just like my friend. I lacked self-love, so I looked to receive love and validation from others. After my divorce, I realized that I needed to take responsibility for my life, that I needed to stop blaming (both my dad and my ex-husband), and that I needed to do the painful work of evolving. Blaming feels good in the moment because it shifts the responsibility off our shoulders and on to someone else. However, blaming leaves us feeling powerless in the long run, whereas taking personal responsibility leaves us feeling empowered. We get to have control over the outcome of our lives. When we blame others, we feel like other people or situations determine the outcome of our lives.

My friend, Julia, a public speaker and comedian, recounted how her lack of self-love and her people-pleasing tendencies ended up contributing to an immense amount of physical pain in her life. She had fallen and landed on her shoulder. She was in so much pain that she could barely move her arm. She went to her doctor and the doctor brushed aside her concerns and told her it was probably just bruised and sore and that she should go home and ice it. Julia knew it was something serious, but so hated confrontation that she didn't even request an x-ray or MRI. She went home and lived with the pain for months. Eventually, she couldn't take the pain any longer and went back to her doctor. The doctor reluctantly sent Julia for x-rays and, as it turned out, she had torn her rotator cuff completely. When we don't love ourselves and advocate for ourselves, we will always deal with undue suffering, whether that be mental, physical, or spiritual.

After my initial conversation with Julia, she sent me the following message and gave me permission to share it with you:

Janice- I have had so many 'revelations' since we spoke. I thought I would update you. It occurred to me that I have been people pleasing since I was a kid. My parents didn't want my sisters or I - we weren't boys, and they made that clear to us. I started the behavior to try to make them like me. I am now scheduled for rotator cuff surgery in a few weeks. What I am finding is that I have done everything for everyone for so long, that I'm having a great deal of difficulty letting go to have the surgery. Even my husband is panicked because I do everything. He is asking for lists of How To's for everything because I have always taken care of it all and now, he'll need to take over. So, a word of caution for anyone who engages in people-pleasing behaviors. One day you could find yourself in a similar situation. Where letting go and allowing others to take over is so stressful that you aren't sure you can do it. These past weeks have been so stressful. I have a full page of things to do prior to my surgery to help my husband take over these tasks that 'just happen' around here. It should never have been like this. I see it now. Just wish I would've seen it earlier.

I wrote back and told Julia that it's never too late to make the necessary changes in our lives. As long as we have breath within us, we can make the decision to learn to value and love ourselves. We can choose to grow in this area.

Part of this growth involves figuring out what you like and dislike, what your values are, and how you want to spend your time. After my divorce, I slowly began to figure out who I was on my own. No one was there to tell me how to do things or when or what or where. I was free to follow my own intuition and listen to myself. I started experimenting with all sorts of things to figure out what I liked doing and how I liked spending my time. I tried different sports. I started interpreting in Spanish. I hung out with different friends. I trained for a marathon. I joined Toastmasters. I started writing poetry and journaling. I began doing yoga regularly. I auditioned for short films. I acted in a play. I competed in a body-building competition. I travelled to exotic places.

Many times, we go through life and then get to a point where we feel like we don't even know who we are or what we like. We become so accustomed to living for other people that we lose touch with ourselves. Women especially fall into this trap. As a general rule, women are nurturers and enjoy caring for others. There is nothing wrong with that. It's actually a beautiful thing as long as we're giving from a place of abundance. We have to make sure our cup is so full that it overflows, because no one can drink from an empty cup.

One of the biggest problems is trying to give from a place of lack. There is a quote that says, "Loving yourself isn't vanity; it's sanity." I couldn't agree more. To stay sane, healthy, and happy, you must practice self-love. When we are good with ourselves and treat ourselves kindly, we can give to others out of a place of abundance rather than trying to "give" from a place of lack. Self-love is the starting point for thriving relationships and positive social impact. Self-love is putting the oxygen mask on yourself first, so that you can then help those around you.

As soon as I realized how important this was, I started to pursue mental and emotional wellness so that I could learn to love myself. I went to pretty much every type of counseling and therapy available. I participated in talk therapy,

EMDR, Neurofeedback, Hypnotherapy, Reiki, and Attachment therapy. I became a certified yoga instructor and a certified hypnosis practitioner.

I was and am a continual student of life. I love learning about mindset and ways to be truly present. I began to see how much I had changed myself to fit what other people expected of me or wanted me to be. I started to notice all the self- hatred I was allowing into my thoughts. I had lost myself, my voice, and who I truly was along the way. If that isn't insanity, I don't know what is! But after hitting rock bottom through the deep loss of my marriage, I was forced to find a different path. This new path was about reclaiming my life. I started doing the things that fulfilled me and started speaking my truth. I also allowed myself to sit with the pain of my past. I looked at it, examined it, dissected it, and reframed it. I sat in stillness connecting to divine presence. I began loving and accepting all the parts of me...the jealous part, the insecure part, the joyful part, the sexual part, the codependent part, the loving part, the feminine part. I learned to embrace the authentic, real me. Only after doing this, was I able to evolve and transform. This process was a rebirth for me. In short, learning to love and accept myself was fundamental to the process of kicking my people-pleasing habit.

A huge part of cultivating self-love is showing up for yourself and keeping the promises you make to yourself. When you do this, you start to develop respect for yourself. You are showing yourself that you are important and valuable enough to follow through on your commitments.

During the infamous quarantine of 2020, I committed to doing Facebook Lives for 30 consecutive days, meaning I had to show up on camera and record myself speaking to the masses. It started off fine. I would get on and talk about random things I was passionate about, tell some stories, or just share a few encouraging words. It was day 28 of 30 of my commitment when George Floyd was murdered. The very last thing I wanted to do was show up on camera and say something. But here's the thing: I HAD MADE A COMMITMENT. I knew that I had to do it or I would be letting myself down. I had enough respect for myself to follow through on my commitment, and although it was hard, I felt proud of myself for keeping my promise. Plus, I was able to share some words of love and solidarity, which I wouldn't have done if l hadn't made that commitment.

Why do we bend over backwards to keep our promises and commitments to other people but don't show up for ourselves? Show yourself how amazing and valuable you are by keeping the promises you make to yourself. Do that exercise class that you promised you'd do. Write in your journal like you said you would. Spend time meditating if you've told yourself that you would. Be mindful of what you commit to and then do your very best to follow through, especially if you've made commitments for your own betterment. Of course, there are going to be moments when you're not going to follow through. You are human, after all! Another important component of self-love is being gracious and forgiving of the times you fall short. Simply accept where you are and do better next time. But whatever you do, always get up and start again! The only time you fail is when you give up completely.

I've known for quite some time that I'm meant to be an inspirational speaker. However, fear held me back from following through on what my intuition already knew. When I was in high school, I forgot the lines of a speech I was giving during a speech competition. I can remember the dozens of eyes staring at me intently. You could hear a pin drop in the room as I stood there searching my mind for words to a speech that I knew like the back of my hand. My mind went completely blank and the silence stretched on and on. Finally, I was able to finish my speech, but I had already ruined my chance of winning. My stomach was tied in knots for weeks afterwards and I felt like such a failure.

That one event caused me to be so fearful that I didn't speak publicly again for about 20 years! For 20 years the fear of failure held me back from doing something I was truly passionate about. After my divorce, I decided to show up differently in life and to walk through all my fears. Once I made that decision, I promised myself that I was going to start speaking publicly again. I went out the next day and joined Toastmasters (a public speaking group) so I could walk through my fear of public speaking. Actually, the fear was never public speaking itself. What I was really afraid of was failing and looking like a fool, just like in high school. I was scared of people's judgment and rejection. I was scared of what others might think about me if I forgot my lines again or failed in some way. And guess what? I did fail again!

During one of my first speeches at Toastmasters, I started shaking uncontrollably. I looked like I was standing out in the middle of Antarctica in shorts and a T-shirt, freezing to death. I even had to hold on to the podium so as to not fall over. I was so embarrassed. I so badly wanted the floor to open up and swallow me whole, but I also knew that this was FEAR showing up, and that if something was going to change in my life, *I* needed to do something different. So instead of sitting down to stabilize myself, I just stood there until the shaking eventually subsided and I continued on with my speech.

This moment was transformational for a couple of reasons: First of all, I looked at my fear head on and faced it. I didn't back down. I walked straight through. It gave me a certain amount of confidence because in my mind it was the worst-case scenario, and yet I was still alive. Nothing seemed to be too altered or damaged because of it. People kept talking to me, the earth continued to spin, and life went on.

Second, people could relate. Many of them came up to me afterwards and told me how encouraged they were by my decision to stay up there and shake instead of sitting down and going back to my comfort zone. It showed them that they too could show up as they were—flawed and imperfect. Walking through your fears matters WAY more than being viewed as "perfect" or "having it all together." When you walk through your fears, you take one step closer to becoming authentically you and living the life you are meant to live. When you show up authentically, you are telling yourself that you are good enough as you are. When you decide to show up without the mask of perfection, you are loving yourself.

Another component of developing self-love is to replace negative self-talk with loving self-talk. My internal dialogue used to consist of things like, "You're ugly" and, "You're despicable and unlovable" and, "You'll never amount to anything." The crazy thing is that I didn't even realize I was constantly telling myself how lame I was! As soon as I became conscious of my internal dialogue, I purposefully started to replace the negative self-talk with positive, uplifting, and empowering messages. I ended up creating an "I am" statement that became my go-to affirmation for myself. My "I am" statement is: "I am a confident, powerful, and purposeful woman."

Try it for yourself. Pick three adjectives and a noun. The adjectives can be characteristics that you would like to embody. They should describe who you WANT to be, even if it feels a far cry from where you are. The present tense "I am" is very important. You are literally speaking this into existence. The more we repeat our empowering "I am" statement, the more it will cement itself into our psyche and we WILL become that person.

Since I didn't feel attractive as a teenager, I was always comparing myself to other girls. I struggled with not feeling beautiful and this belief deeply impacted my self-confidence. Many women struggle with comparing their appearance to someone else's. This can lead to feeling jealous, insecure, and depressed. I've struggled with feelings of jealousy, so much so that it seemed to reside within me at the deepest level.

> *Can jealousy sit in your bones?*
> *Because I swear jealousy sits in my bones.*
> *It sits and waits, quietly, patiently, until that, there! Some trigger sets it off.*
> *And the jealousy gets restless from sitting so long in my bones.*
> *It jumps to attention and gets ready for a full-frontal attack.*
> *Its sole intent is to destroy, to divide and conquer.*
> *It is ruthless and takes no prisoners, annihilating everything in its path.*
> *It leaves me feeling small and worthless and pathetic.*
> *And then, once completely satiated, it settles back down and sits in my bones.*

These feelings of insecurity, jealousy, and lack can feel completely overpowering. However, you can slowly shift these emotions by changing the way you view yourself, talk to yourself, and treat yourself. You get to choose to love and accept yourself just as you are. View yourself as royalty. Talk to yourself as you would your favorite person in the whole world. Treat yourself with compassion and grace. Toss shame, guilt, and criticisms out the window. They will only hold you back and impede your progress. Instead, lean into surrender, forgiveness, and gratitude.

Loving ourselves comes from knowing deep down that, at our core, we are perfect love. We get separated from that love during our lives. Wounds, fears, hurt, thoughts, and trauma all come in and put up a wall between us and who we truly are. Our mission on this earth is to return to this love and to our true essence. Take some time to sit in stillness, remember who you truly are, and always come back to love.

"Sometimes your soulmate is yourself. You have to be the love of your life, until you discover that love in someone else." - r.h. Sin

Step # 3:
Cultivate and Develop Self-Love

STEP 4

Establish
Boundaries

Step 4
Establish Boundaries

No.

Say it with me: No.

Did you know that "No" is a complete sentence? I was completely uncomfortable with this concept when I first heard it.

Saying "no" and establishing boundaries is one of the hardest things for people pleasers. We are supposed to be pleasing people and making them happy, and rarely does refusing to do what the person wants bring them joy. In fact, it will usually create distress. However, this is a great way to start taking your power back and establishing your own personal identity.

Setting boundaries comes from knowing what is acceptable to you and what is unacceptable.

Boundaries come from knowing yourself, knowing your values, and knowing how you want to live your life. They also come from listening to your intuition. This means the ability to understand something immediately, without the need for conscious reasoning.

As toddlers, we tend to be really good about setting boundaries. If we didn't want to do something, we would very emphatically say or yell "no!" However, as we get older, our main focus is to fit in and be accepted, so we start turning down the volume on our "no." We want to feel loved and we don't want to be left out. Lots of teenagers can attest to being talked into drinking, smoking, having sex, skipping school, even engaging in criminal activity, simply because they want to fit in and belong.

I was pretty good about setting boundaries in high school. Being raised in the church, I had certain values that I held to, and I mostly hung out with other kids from my church, who shared similar values. The church made it easy to know what was acceptable and what wasn't; I felt comfortable in that environment. It wasn't until after I got married that I really upped my people-pleasing game. I wanted so desperately to make my husband happy. In a sense, I idolized him. Many times, people pleasing and codependency (excessive emotional or psychological reliance on a partner) go hand-in-hand.

I spent a lot of time doing things for my husband and apologizing. He demanded; I conceded. I didn't want to rock the boat or argue with him. I am a pretty stubborn person, but I can truly say that he broke me. Just like water creates deep canyons after years of running over rocks, he wore me down. After many years, I had no more fight left in me. This is how I came to be in the position of doing sexual activities that I had no interest in doing. This is how I came to pushing aside my values and ignoring my intuition. I knew it was not what I wanted to do, and it was not in me to give, YET I DID IT ANYWAY. I did it because I feared his rejection. I didn't have enough confidence or belief in myself to set clear boundaries and stick to them. So, how do we establish boundaries?

First, we need to know what boundaries are right for us. This only becomes clear when we really know ourselves. Many times, it takes some experimentation, as well as trial and error. Welcome to the School of Life! We need to establish our values and beliefs, not just accept what we were taught as children. Just because you were taught something as a child doesn't necessarily mean it is in alignment with how you truly feel or the beliefs you want to adopt as an adult. Many people don't take the time to reevaluate these subjects and unconsciously take whatever they learned as a child into adulthood.

Consider whether your current thoughts and beliefs are serving you or if they are limiting you and holding you back. A good example of this is someone's beliefs about money. Maybe when growing up they were taught that making a lot of money was evil. Instead of reconsidering whether they actually think this is true, they continue thinking money is bad and live with a scarcity mindset. The crazy thing is that many times we aren't aware that we have adopted these kinds of beliefs. They are deeply rooted in our subconscious.

My mom was codependent, an enabler, and a people pleaser in her relationship with my dad. I learned how to operate that way in my own life by following her example. It wasn't until a few years ago that I realized I had created the exact type of dynamic in the relationship with my husband as she had with my dad. Think about your own parents/guardians and what you learned by watching their example. Were their behaviors healthy and loving or were they dysfunctional? Give yourself permission to keep what serves you and discard the rest.

After we have checked in with our intuition and reevaluated our personal values and beliefs, we can start setting boundaries with others. It is a good idea to be clear and assertive when communicating your boundaries. We don't want to be aggressive, but we do need to be assertive. Assertive language is clear and non-negotiable without attacking or blaming the other person. One of the best ways to start this type of conversation is with an "I feel..." statement. No one can argue with how you feel, and you are also not pointing the finger at someone else when using this verbiage.

A great assertive statement will look something like this: "I feel _____ when because _____. What I need is _____."

This type of sentence is perfect because you are expressing **how you feel, why you feel it, and what you need.** It is clear and unambiguous. It may be hard to formulate these sentences and express them at first, but the more you practice, the easier it will become.

Two years after my divorce, I met a man at Toastmasters (he was lucky enough to witness my shaking incident, LOL). This man intrigued me after he gave a speech about taking personal responsibility for his health situation (he was on dialysis at the time). We began talking more and eventually started dating. After a few months, I asked him if he watched porn. He said that he did, and I immediately knew that I could not allow that behavior in my life again. I needed to set a clear, firm boundary. I sat down and wrote him this letter:

Pornography is a deal breaker for me. I have seen and continue to see its negative consequences in the people I love and in the world as a whole. It takes something so beautiful, so deep, so majestic, and turns it into something so common, so trashy, so disposable. I think the effect that it has on the brain of a man is nothing short of catastrophic. Images and thoughts that cannot be taken back. There they remain seared forever in the brain and in the heart. It is exactly like a drug. A high, instant pleasure, gratification that doesn't need to be worked for or earned. And then it is gone, and there one remains, a little bit hardened (no pun intended), the wall between himself and the outside world solidified a bit more, an eye and a heart that is looking, searching for fulfillment that cannot be found in the direction in which he is gazing. And then the cycle repeats and repeats itself.

Pornography has negatively impacted my life and so many of the lives of people I know, yours included. When I've watched it, I've liked parts of it and it turns me on, so I certainly don't mean to sound like I'm superior or better than. However, I know that it is destructive and for this reason I want no part of it. I don't want to watch it, I don't want it in my home, and I definitely don't want it in the heart of the man I'm seeing and opening myself up to.

Step 4: Establish Boundaries

I am looking for something more. I am looking for a man who respects women enough to know that looking at them just to satisfy himself, is the opposite of respect. A man who is willing to do the hard work of earning satisfaction and release and not looking for the easiest way to have a quick feel-good moment. One who values all women and therefore would not dream of looking at them as an object, just to please himself. A man who sees the unhealthy and destructive ways that pornography invades the hearts and minds of those watching and detaches sex from what it was meant to be.

If you are that man, please let me know. Also, if you are not that man, it is very important that I know that as well. I will not judge you either way. I will simply know whether we are on the same path or not. If you decide that you are that man, then I only ask one thing of you. Please tell me if you change your mind and decide that you are not that man. Please don't ever do anything behind my back and keep it from me. I am strong and can deal with many things. However, being lied to, whether it be a bold-faced lie or a lie of omission, is also a deal breaker and something that I have no ounce of tolerance left in me to give. Think all of this over and then let me know what you decide. I'm not interested in prolonging our relationship if we are not on the same page, walking similar paths. It just doesn't make sense.

To end this very serious letter, I will confess something to you. I confess that you have shown me what sex is meant to be. I honestly never knew I could feel so loved, so valued, so taken care of, and so desired in sex. Now that I know how it is meant to be, I can never go back to anything else. And I have you to thank for that. So, whatever your decision about the porn stuff, know that I am forever grateful to you for showing me the deep, beautiful, intimate, and soulful type of sex that I have always longed for. I wouldn't have been able to dream it up any better than it is.

Remember that when setting boundaries, it is helpful to express how you feel, why you feel it, and what you need. In my opinion, honesty is the best policy. Allow yourself to be truly seen. Secondly, we need to practice using the word "no." When establishing new boundaries, I suggest starting small. Practice saying no and setting boundaries with people you don't know well and care less about and work your way to those closest to you. This will be uncomfortable. DO IT ANYWAY. You can ease into it by using phrases such as, "No, that won't work for me." Or, "I'd like to help, but I have a prior commitment." Or, "I don't think that will work, but let me think on it a little bit."

Once you've eased yourself into declining invites/requests with these phrases, try just saying "no." Force yourself to say no without having to offer an excuse or make something up. As a general principal, we don't like feeling uncomfortable and awkward. When we say no without a justification, we tend to feel like we're being rude. It is important to remember that, by setting boundaries, you are creating a life you love, and that being honest and true to yourself is actually fortifying to the relationship. It is your job to teach people how to treat you.

Another people-pleasing trait is apologizing for no good reason way too often. Saying sorry is great when we really mean it and we've actually done something wrong. However, there are many times we say "sorry" out of habit, and it's simply not necessary. I saw a meme the other day that outlined what we could say instead of constantly apologizing:

INSTEAD OF...	TRY...
Sorry I'm late	Thank you for waiting
Sorry I messed up	I'll fix that now
Sorry I bumped into you	Excuse me
Sorry to bother you	Do you have a minute?
Sorry I didn't understand XYZ	Can you help me understand XYZ?

Notice how the second sentences feel better when saying them and are more empowering. It's taken me a long time to realize that the words I speak are a reflection of the thoughts I think. With enough repetition, we can retrain our brains. Next time you're tempted to say "I'm sorry" off the cuff, stop and think if the situation truly merits an apology or if there's a better way to express what you really mean.

Lastly, when setting boundaries, we must be prepared to upset the other person. We need to be strong and brave enough to handle conflict. We may even encounter some situations where we need to step away from the relationship for some time or end it altogether.

A few years ago, I encountered a situation where I had to set boundaries and eventually end a relationship. I had been invited to go with three women to walk the Camino de Santiago in Spain. I didn't know any of them. I'm all about adventure, and so I immediately said "yes!" The plan was for the three of us to go on practice walks to get to know each other while simultaneously making sure our bodies could get used to walking for hours upon hours. The woman who had organized it (let's call her Laurie) was of high repute and well-known in the community. She was a speaker and writer and was frequently on the radio and other media outlets. After a few practice walks, I began to notice the controlling nature this woman possessed. She would tell us how to respond to certain situations and how to feel or not feel. It really started to concern me. The other two women and I started to second-guess our responses to her and it felt like we were walking on eggshells around her.

After careful consideration, I decided that I needed to call a meeting to discuss how I was feeling and air out my concerns. I sent out an email to all three of them, saying I'd like to meet and talk. Laurie (probably accurately guessing that it was about her) ignored my email and went behind my back trying to get the other two women on her side. The way Laurie was acting was shocking to me. I knew that I couldn't walk for miles on end in her presence while being kind and true to myself at the same time.

I ended up sending them all an email telling them that I would not be going on the walk with them after all. I was really nervous to send out that email knowing that Laurie would be angry and the other two women disappointed. Part of me thought I would just suck it up and ignore the way she was treating us, and be a martyr about it, but at this point I was changing and growing. My awareness started to kick in; I realized that my time was too valuable to spend it in misery, being controlled by another human being. I knew I needed to surround myself with people who were uplifting, kind, and loving. And I needed to eliminate toxic, controlling, judgmental people from my life (or at least limit my interactions with them). I was finally learning how to stand up for myself, how to love myself, and how to value my time and energy.

It ended up being the best decision. I still went to walk the Camino, but I did it with my dear friend, Julie, who is loving, encouraging, and so much fun! The other two women still went with Laurie, and they ended up having a miserable time (I later found out). They eventually split from Laurie during their journey, and the two of them met up with my friend and me for a nice dinner in Spain. It was a learning and growing experience for all of us. I haven't spoken with Laurie since, but I hope that by all three of us setting boundaries with her she was able to evolve in her own life journey.

Setting boundaries is a gift to us and to the other person. For us, it is valuing ourselves enough to tell others how we wish to be treated. We feel more genuine love and joy when we say "yes" from a place free from obligation, guilt, and fear. Those yeses will be meaningful and honest. Saying no will allow for that. For the other person, it is setting very clear rules for them to abide by to be in a relationship with us. There is no second-guessing or ambiguity. They can then choose whether they want to be in the relationship with us or not.

After my divorce, I self-published a book called *Bits & Pieces of a Broken Heart* to speak out and tell my story. I wrote about and disclosed some family secrets that had to do with my dad. Before I published it, I sat down with him and let him know that I would be publishing a book about my life, and my life just happened to include things about him as my dad. This was one of the hardest things I've done because I was facing my dad's possible anger, sadness, and disapproval. I had to accept the fact that in order to tell my story, to be honest and authentic, I could very well lose my relationship with my dad. Dad/daughter relationships are important, and I was really struggling with disclosing this information to him.

My heart was pounding when we had the conversation, but I was committed to living authentically. I had come to the point of doing what I needed to do to break the people-pleasing habit even if that meant letting go of certain relationships. I knew it was necessary for healing my wounds and standing in my own power. My dad was disappointed and sad, but accepted that I needed to do what I felt was right for me -- and our relationship continues to this day. Since then, I've had to establish other boundaries with my dad, and although it causes him discomfort, he chooses to continue having a relationship with me and I with him.

The bottom line is that we have to be willing to change or lose relationships with others to be true to ourselves. By doing this, we will also find our tribe of people who support and love the real us. The toxic relationships will leave, allowing room for the positive, healthy ones to take root. I'm not saying you have to throw everyone out of your life! But I am saying to notice and be aware of the people who help you grow and the ones who keep you stuck. Notice if they boost your energy or drain it. Make adjustments as far as how much time you spend with them and how much you allow them into your inner circle.

This is a good time to make a list of the people closest to you. Write down all the names and think about how you feel around each person. Consider whether you feel positive and joyful after spending time with them, or burdened and negative. The people you choose to surround yourself with matter immensely. We can find these people by setting boundaries in our lives. These boundaries protect us from energy drainers and toxicity, and conversely, allow us to bring in light, love, and positivity.

Warren Buffet, an investor and philanthropist, rightfully said:

> *"Surround yourself with people who push you to do and be better. No drama or negativity. Just higher goals and higher motivation. Good times and positive energy. No jealousy or hate. Simply bringing out the absolute best in each other."*

Step #4:
Establish Boundaries

STEP 5

Decide and Do

Step 5
Decide and Do

I knew the family secrets were poison to my soul. I could feel it. My dad's past had caught up to him, and now those burdens lay heavily at my feet. The sexual molestation, the underage encounters, the double life he led felt like a large weight on my shoulders. Some of our extended family knew about his past indiscretions, but it was mostly a hush-hush type of situation.

After my divorce, I decided *I* was the one who needed to change. I needed to show up differently in life. So instead of sweeping my thoughts and feelings under the rug, as was my usual MO, I decided to open up and share about my life. My dad could choose to deflect and lie and manipulate, but I also had a choice. So, I decided to be honest and open about my past, which involved sharing about my dad's double life and the sexual dynamic between me and my husband. I decided to do this, but then I froze. It was really, really scary to put certain things out there. I was paralyzed by my fear of people's opinions. I was scared of what people would say about me and how they would view me. I was scared of being judged negatively or thought of poorly. I also felt this need to protect my dad. Even though he had made poor decisions and hurt those closest to him, I still felt as though it was my job to make him happy and not rock the boat. All of these same feelings applied to my ex-husband as well.

However, deep down I knew that I needed to express these truths and I needed to share my story. I decided to put it all out there and allow myself to be seen. The thing about deciding to change, whether that means not falling into the trap of people pleasing or choosing to face your fears, is that it involves taking action. It's not enough to simply decide and commit to changing. One must follow through on those decisions and commitments in the form of DOING.

Through the experience of publishing my previous book, I learned that people will judge based on their own views of the world, their own experiences, and their own mindset. It really has nothing to do with me or my story. It has everything to do with them and their thoughts, beliefs, and wounds. I had a relative write to me and tell me I was making a mistake by divorcing my husband.

She didn't know the whole story and was projecting her experiences and beliefs onto me. But instead of falling into my familiar people-pleasing behaviors, a new perspective came to me. I realized that her story was not my story, and her truth was not my truth. I started to learn how to disconnect from other people's projections and opinions without being upset with them. I began to discover how to not take things personally.

Decide and commit to kicking the people-pleasing habit for YOU. You will never, ever, ever be able to make every single person think highly of you or like you or agree with you. No matter what you do! Mother Teresa has critics. Jesus has critics. Gandhi has critics. Decide and commit to change your life, for you. Step out of your comfort zone so that you can evolve and become the best version of yourself, for you. People pleasing doesn't get you what you want in life. If anything, it harms you. It keeps you from your best self, and from giving and receiving the love you deserve. I know it's a terrifying concept, but you will never be able to make every single person think highly of you. However, once you love yourself completely, you won't need to have everyone like and approve of you. It will become irrelevant.

To kick the people-pleasing habit, it's helpful to have a compelling reason or a strong enough why. My strong and compelling reason to change was that my marriage had fallen apart right before my eyes, and I still needed to live and move about in this world. I had two young children who were counting on me to hold it together and give them all that they needed. Even during the days when I had to drag myself out of bed, exhausted from being up at night crying and lamenting my life, I had to take care of those two beautiful, dependent creatures. They were my *why* at first. I had to be there for them. I couldn't bail out on life just because I was now alone. I had to get up, take care of everyday life, and provide for them. Eventually, my *why* became the love I began to develop for myself. I started to love myself enough that I knew I couldn't settle for anything less ever again.

In order to really follow through, your reason and motivation for changing has to be worthy of your commitment. And then, you must decide that you will do what it takes to create a better type of existence for yourself. You are worthy of that goal. Before we get into creating a better existence for yourself, let's consider the consequences of you continuing along this people-pleasing rut.

As a people pleaser, you will never experience a full, happy life because you will be bound by what other people think of you. You will not be authentically who you truly are. You will lose your voice. You will forever wear a mask. You will become a shell of a person. You will be like a boat without a rudder, blown about in every which way, tossed in every direction, with no clear compass or destination in mind. You will read, and re-read, and edit, and then eventually delete a simple text message because you will fret about how the person you're sending it to will interpret it. You will stifle your unique abilities. You will take care of everyone but yourself. You will support others at the expense of your own well- being. You will be surrounded by takers -- those who can sense your need for their approval and will latch onto you and suck your energy, your time, and your love away from you. They will drain the life out of you. You will eventually resent them. You will ignore them, and then feel guilty and reach back out. You will not be living the life you were meant to live.

My friend and fellow actress, Angela Barber, met with me to talk about her experiences with people pleasing. Because of her own emotional wounds, she began pleasing others to get a sense of self-worth and importance. She felt that she needed to be perfect in all areas of her life. She needed to have the perfect appearance, the perfect man, the perfect home, the perfect family, and throw to the most perfect parties. It became difficult for her to keep up the image of perfection all the time, so she began drinking alcohol to help her cope. She did what everyone wanted her to do and eventually people started expecting her to always come through, to always say yes, and to always pick up their slack. She was pushed to the edge and the drinking got worse and worse to the point of missing a whole month of work. At that point, she was able to acknowledge that she was a mess and that her life was crumbling down around her. The people pleasing and perfectionism, as well as the constant drinking, resulted in Angela checking in to rehab.

Angela did the 12-step recovery program and has been sober for 10 years now. She is pursuing a mental health counseling degree. She made the decision to change, and then followed through with actions. She is doing the work. She reads books, goes to counseling, does research, and educates herself so that she can continue with the process of her own personal evolution. She makes time for herself and allows herself to regenerate and refuel. She is true to herself now, and the more she is true to herself, the more she feels a desire to make an impact in the world. She wants to help others who are struggling like she once was. Although she is thriving now, at one point in her life the consequences of people pleasing were quite evident. She left me with a quote that sent chills down my spine. She said, "Let's not light ourselves on fire to make others feel warm."

Psychotherapist, speaker, and author Dr. Anne Brown also described the consequences of people pleasing amazingly well:

"There is a huge cost to your soul: no dignity, no honesty, no opinions and thoughts of your own, and no you, are just some of the costs."

You don't want that type of life for yourself. You are worthy of cultivating and developing love from within. Breaking the habit of people pleasing starts with deciding—deciding you will learn how to stop devoting your life to pleasing others so that you can focus on your own truth and authenticity. This will result in true kindness and pure love. And it all comes down to a choice.

Beloved children's book author, Dr. Suess, said it brilliantly when he wrote:

"You have brains in your head. You have feet in your shoes. You can steer yourself in any direction you choose. You're on your own. And you know what you know. And YOU are the one who will decide where to go."

Close your eyes and think about who you wanted to be when you grew up. Who did you see? What did you picture yourself doing? What excited you and made you feel alive and vibrant? It was so easy to dream and envision as children. Maybe you wanted to be an astronaut or a secretary. Maybe a singer or dancer. And usually what you wanted to be was accompanied by a feeling. Feeling important or feeling beautiful or feeling smart or feeling free.

As adults we lose the ability to dream big because of our fear of failure. We are scared that we won't be able to achieve or accomplish something, and so we don't even try. It's time to decide that we are going to live this one life we have fully and unapologetically. Decide that you no longer want to feel responsible for everybody and their mother. Decide that you are no longer responsible for other people's happiness or well- being. Decide to love yourself first and foremost. When you do that, the love within you spills over onto everything and everyone around you. And it is pure, true love. It doesn't need a thing. It has no expectations and no conditions. At that point you can give and give and give and there's no resentment because the love you are extending is coming from a place of overflowing abundance. It comes from a place of authenticity and truth.

The reason we don't take action is because we get stuck in a fear state. Fear of failure holds us all back from moving forward. We stay stuck and paralyzed because our comfort zone feels so safe. However, know that everything purposeful, beautiful, fulfilling, exciting, and valuable lies outside your comfort zone.

I recently read about Epictetus, a Greek philosopher. He came up with a concept he called "The Sphere of Choice." He believed that there are things which are within our power (internals) and things which are beyond our power (externals). Internals are things we can control such as our perceptions, opinions, reactions, and passions. Externals are things outside of our control such as other people's opinions, nature, events, and disasters. The key is to focus on the internals and let go of the externals. Focus on the things you CAN control instead of focusing on the things you CAN'T control.

If you choose to focus on the internals, you can move from fear of failure to full on freedom. Make the choice to take your power back! ***It is helpful to realize that you must fail in order to succeed.*** When we were babies learning to walk, we fell often, until one day we were able to take our first steps. Babies don't give up because they fall. They cry, dust themselves off, and get up and try again and again and again. It would do us all well to return to that toddler mindset of constantly getting back up and not giving up. As adults, we get stuck because we are fearful of what others will think about us if we fail or lose or don't get something exactly right.

The famous basketball player, Michael Jordan, said something incredibly powerful. It's one of my favorite quotes of all time. He said:

"I've missed more than 9,000 shots in my career. I've lost almost 300 games. Twenty-six times I've been trusted to take the game winning shot and missed. I've failed over and over and over again in my life. And that is why I succeed."

BAM!!!! That quote fires me up! We have to be willing to fail. Go messy early. Lay it all out there. Banish perfectionism from your life. Be seen! Live fully! Love deeply!

In order to change our people-pleasing ways, we must commit to changing ourselves. It's a tall order, but it's imperative. Change is never easy. More often than not, people would rather stay in less-than-ideal circumstances than have to face the unknown. This is why, many times, women who are abused stay with their abusers. It's a horrible situation, but at least they know what to expect.

My advice to changing yourself is to start small. If we set a huge goal, it's easy to become overwhelmed. Therefore, we need to take some serious baby steps in the beginning.

Diane Rolston, life coach, author, and speaker, wrote about the irrelevance of the size of the goal:

"The size of the goal has no relation to the power it has to move you forward in confidence and growth."

Small steps are good because they don't overload our brains and they leverage a positive feedback loop (when we accomplish things, we feel good). We gain momentum, and it becomes easier to keep going. It also strengthens our confidence and trust in ourselves and our abilities. We want these small steps that we take to turn into healthy habits. The best way to get habits to stick is to start small and do whatever the new behavior is every day for three to four weeks straight. It is also helpful to stack a new habit on top of an existing habit.

As part of working on my self-love, I started taking small steps to create healthier physical and mental habits for myself. Here is one example of starting small and stacking habits: I love my coffee. I wake up in the morning and it's usually the first thing I think about. I allow myself one cup in the morning, but I try to keep it at one cup a day. I started to notice that my body didn't really like having coffee be the first thing inside its stomach each morning, and I had read somewhere that starting your day off with warm lemon water was great for detoxing the body and helping the digestive system get off to a good start. I decided that I wanted to start off my day with lemon water and *then* treat myself to a cup of coffee. I've tied these two habits together. Think of what current habit you have that you can attach a new habit to. For example, when you're in the shower, it could be a great time to do a quick visualization, or when you're brushing your teeth, you can silently repeat empowering affirmations to yourself.

A tool I use when creating new, healthier habits, is to think of it as replacing instead of eliminating. No one wants to feel deprived, even if deprivation is a mere state of mind. We want to feel abundant and satisfied, happy and full. Think of new habits as simply replacing one way of doing something with another way. Replacing victim mentality with an empowered mentality. Replacing criticism with praise. Replacing fear with love. Replacing chips with carrots. Replacing complaining with gratitude. Replacing stagnation with movement. Replacing alcohol with water. Replacing blame with personal responsibility. Our daily habits define us, so let us create habits that are in alignment with our best selves. You get to choose and create these new, empowering habits!

Another helpful component in achieving goals and creating healthy habits is to have accountability. One of the first things I decided to do after my divorce was to run a marathon. I committed to running one for several reasons. First, I thought it was an impossible thing to accomplish since I hated running and could barely run around the block, so I wanted to prove to myself that I could accomplish something seemingly impossible. Second, I needed to spend my time doing good things for myself since there were days I was so miserable that I didn't even want to get out of bed. I needed a goal and something to work toward.

The very first thing I did was sign up to train with a running group. I knew I needed support and motivation if I was ever going to accomplish this feat. The group met three times a week; one of those times was at 7am on Saturday. I've never really enjoyed waking up early, especially not to go out and run for miles on end. However, I decided and committed to running the marathon, and I knew that I couldn't just show up in four months without training and run it. I knew I needed to take small, consistent steps toward my goal. If you are consistent enough, in whatever you do, you will be blown away by the final result. Tears of joy threatened to stream down my face when I finally crossed the finish line after completing a goal that I had previously thought was impossible.

This one moment was a huge step toward creating a new life for myself. Instead of a people pleaser who lived from a place of fear, I had become an independent woman who could set difficult goals and follow through in accomplishing them. I was beginning to reclaim my life. I was slowly coming back to myself.

When you decide to change, you will need to take action to follow through on your decision and commitment. A commitment without action is like a car without gas; it's useless.

John Boyd, creator of the OODA Loop (Observe, Orient, Decide, Act), once said:

"Decisions without actions are pointless. Actions without decisions are reckless."

Decisions and actions go hand in hand. What decisions can you make and what actions can you take to move you further away from people pleasing and closer to living your own amazing, authentic life? What decisions and actions will move you toward your dreams and toward your best life? Whatever those are, they are worth your time, energy, effort, and focus.

When I made the decision to change, I came face-to-face with my past. I had to revisit my dad's double life. I had to deal with my feelings of abandonment and emotional neglect from my mom. I had to really examine my lack of self-worth that led me to going against my values in my marriage. I had to look at how I tended to show up as everyone else wanted me to be instead of how I truly was. I had to acknowledge that I was stuck in a state of fear and felt paralyzed to move forward. I had to come face-to-face with the darkest parts of myself. My decision to face the pain of it all and then take action to create a new mindset for myself was the beginning of my healing and peace. I'm certain it will be the same for you.

"All great changes are preceded by chaos."
– Deepak Chopra

Step # 5:
Decide and Do

STEP 6

Envision & Step
Into Your Highest Self

Step 6
Envision & Step Into Your Highest Self

*"If you don't know where you're going,
you'll end up someplace else."*
— Yogi Berra

*"The only thing worse than being blind
is having sight but no vision."*
— Helen Keller

*"A man without a vision for his future
will always return to his past."*
— Anonymous

*"The vision must be followed by the venture.
It is not enough to stare up the steps—
we must step up the stairs."*
— Vance Havner

When I was younger, I didn't have much of a vision for my life. It felt scary to dream big or to think that I would be capable of making those dreams a reality. Also, true to the ways of people pleasers, I didn't express my opinions about anything. The safest bet was for me to agree with everyone and keep any dissenting views to myself. This way of operating started impacting my life in ways I didn't even realize. When asked where I wanted to go to dinner, I would just say, "I'm good with anything. You decide." When asked what movie I wanted to see, my answer would be the same. I was a doormat, a "yes" person, and a woman without a vision.

We cannot create something we can't envision. We cannot become someone we don't think is possible to become. Before stepping into the greatness of who you truly are, you must be able to see it in your mind's eye. When visualizing the highest version of yourself, you must have your end goal in mind. Who are you as the highest version of yourself? What adjectives describe you? How do you feel? How are you showing up in the world?

To kick the people-pleasing habit, you will need to create a new vision for yourself and your life. Bury the old and give birth to the new.

- The old version of yourself looks to others to give you approval. **The new version looks within.**

- The old version moves through life aimlessly, blown about depending upon external circumstances. **The new version is on a path of your own choosing, where you decide which turn to take and which direction to go.**

- The old version of yourself keeps quiet because you fear letting someone down. **The new version speaks your truth in a loving, assertive way.**

- The old version is surrounded by takers and emotional vampires. **The new version is intentional about being surrounded by those who truly want the best for you and help you to grow.**

Close your eyes. Can you envision the new you?

As I stated before, the first time I had a vision of the highest version of myself was during a hypnotherapy session. I saw myself standing on a cliff overlooking the ocean. I was looking out into the horizon. I had a long, white, flowing dress on and was standing with my shoulders back and my heart forward. I noticed my face was completely relaxed with no sign of tension or stress. There was a slight smile on my face, and I felt peaceful, calm, powerful, and purposeful. I knew that I was seeing and feeling the best version of me that lay buried underneath the fears, doubts, insecurities, and trauma. That confident woman on the cliff was me indeed!

The woman I envisioned on the cliff was a far cry from how I previously saw myself, which was more like a drowned rat. I literally had this mental image of myself soaking wet, covered in mud, stringy hair covering my face with my shoulders hunched forward and eyes downcast. This drowned rat image embodied my insecurities and lack of self-love. I had seen myself in that way for as long as I could remember. It definitely was not me as my best and highest self.

Author, yoga instructor, and incredible human being Megan Morgan shared with me the vision she had of her highest self. During her Reiki training, she visualized herself out in space. She saw a crossed legged figure made of stars in the distance. Light was going through its body and as she stared at it, it got brighter and brighter. It looked like a fountain of energy and light. She walked closer and closer and as she approached it, she realized that it was actually her. She recognized that this entity sitting in front of her was her highest self. She had the feeling that everything was so much bigger and grander than just what's happening on earth. She felt a knowing and centeredness that she had never experienced before.

In large part due of this vision, Megan has been able to step outside of any fear or people-pleasing tendencies she once had to create a vibrant life for herself in which she allows her intuition and creativity to guide her. She has started a podcast, written a book, and teaches yoga as a means to positively influence and connect to the world. She intentionally thinks about the vision she once had of her highest self when she feels uncertain or fearful.

Being able to visualize your highest self is important because it allows you to take the necessary steps to become who you are meant to be. Seeing who you truly are makes it possible to embody those attributes. You can then begin taking small, yet consistent, steps toward it. Once you have visualized your highest self, you can return to that image/feeling time and time again when you are feeling discouraged, defeated, and lacking. Even recalling the memory of the visualization will release endorphins and "feel good" chemicals throughout your body.

The image of my highest self was so important to me that I hired my friend, Nafsheen Luhar, a photographer and painter, to recreate my visualization and paint it on a canvas for me. So now, I have a large painting of myself, standing on top of a cliff overlooking the ocean, hanging in my bedroom. It is there to remind me daily of who

I truly am -- because I often forget. Not everyone will want to hire someone to paint their highest self, but it is important to document it in some way. Write down your visualizations so that you can easily go back and remind yourself of your true nature and your best self.

Not only do we have the power to visualize our highest selves, we also can visualize accomplishing goals and conquering fears. There are many successful people who credit much of their success to visualization. I love the story of Jim Carrey, who as a struggling actor, decided to write himself a check for $10 million for "acting services rendered" and kept it in his pocket for inspiration. Four years later, Carrey earned exactly $10 million for his role in *Dumb and Dumber*. How cool is that?! Many athletes and celebrities attribute their success to the power of visualization.

It's a good idea to set aside five minutes or so each day (doing this in the shower is a great way to stack your habits) and visualize how you want to show up in the world as the best version of yourself. Make sure the visualization is something achievable and believable. I have started to visualize myself on a stage speaking in front of large audiences. I visualize exactly what I'm wearing, how I'm feeling, what I'm talking about, how the audience is receiving what I'm saying, and so forth.

Since I've struggled with shaking while speaking, I visualize myself being very grounded and centered and feeling solid and secure.

Once you have this vision of the best and brightest version of yourself, how do you go about actually becoming this person? The answer is paradoxical. You sit in stillness and then you get to work! You balance the silence and stillness with movement and action. In yoga, we are taught to balance effort with ease. Holding the postures requires effort and strength, but simultaneously we want to breathe deeply and relax muscles that aren't being used for that posture, such as the muscles in our face. It's living in flow. We are doing, but we are also allowing. We are not forcing or controlling. We are like water, moving seamlessly around and over and under all the obstacles placed in our way.

I love this quote by the ancient Chinese philosopher and writer, Lao Tzu:

"Search your heart and see. The way to do is to be."

To accomplish our best work and put in 100% effort, we must learn how to simply be. Practicing meditation is a great way to tune in to ourselves and learn to be in the present moment, as well as how to live in a more relaxed, flowing state. By focusing on our breath, or other bodily sensations, we can start to notice how we are separate from our thoughts. We start to realize that our thoughts do not define us. We begin to take control back from our own minds.

Try this exercise.

Sit in a comfortable position and close your eyes. Begin to imagine that you are sitting on a bench in a train station. Your only job is to sit on the bench and observe the trains coming and going into the station. The first train pulls in, and you watch as people get off and on and then you watch it pull away from the station. After this, there is no activity whatsoever for some time. You remain seated and observe the silence and stillness. You take some deep breaths. Then, you notice another train pulling into the station. Again, you sit and observe the train. You don't get up off the bench to board the train. You simply sit and watch. You observe with curiosity. No judgement, simply curiosity.

Now, imagine that the trains are your thoughts. Each time you have a thought, you notice that you are having a thought. You observe it, but you don't cling to the thought or let the thought carry you away. You don't board the train. Your only job is to notice it and then let it exit your mind, let it leave the train station. Many times, we allow our thoughts to carry us to mental places that are not healthy for us. One thought, if we allow it, can take us to other negative, unhealthy thoughts and before we know it, we are an anxious wreck or in a depressed state of mind. Choose to observe your thoughts and then release them. This takes a lot of practice and dedication.

In 2016, I went to Hawaii for a two-week yoga teacher training. Part of this training was sitting still in the morning and meditating. Our yoga instructor told us that when our minds started to drift, we should label the thought we were having, such as judging, reminiscing, questioning, analyzing. And then, immediately go back to focusing on our breath. It allowed me to notice how many thoughts I had and also how many of those thoughts were negative and judgmental (toward myself and others). I truly became aware that I am NOT my thoughts. I am the consciousness underneath them. You are the consciousness underneath your thoughts as well. Practice (through meditation) separating yourself from your thoughts. I love this quote that I heard from a friend of mine:

> *"You are not your first thought. You are your second thought and your first action."*

Thoughts come and go. Focus on creating and choosing the thoughts that serve you and let the rest go.

Here are a few ways to practice
"BE"ing:

- Take time to sit in silence.
- Meditate.
- Focus on your breath.
- Do yoga.
- Stretch your muscles.
- Take a leisurely walk.
- Lie down and intentionally relax your muscles one by one.
- Close your eyes and listen to the sounds around you.
- Place your hand on your heart and connect to it.
- Focus on opening your heart.
- Pause between tasks.
- Notice your internal landscape (thoughts, feelings, tension).
- Write in a journal anything that comes to mind. Do not edit or analyze.
- Take a break from electronic devices.
- Watch the clouds drift by.
- Take a nap.
- Float in a pool or river.

If we are constantly trying to fill our days and hours with non-stop activity and connection to our phones, we are missing out on a key ingredient for becoming the best, happiest, most fulfilled versions of ourselves. Schedule time alone. Put your quiet times and meditation times in your calendar. Prioritize it. We somehow think that we will find the time, but if you're anything like me, it will fall through the cracks or get pushed to the back burner. Exhaustion and burnout occur when we continue to go full throttle. It's much better to be proactive than reactive. If you don't take time for your physical and mental health, you will be forced to take time for your sickness and panic attacks. Take time for yourself, just like you would for a friend or family member. You and your well-being are important and deserve to be treated as such! When you feel grounded and peaceful emotionally, this will translate into you being a more loving and supportive person to those around you.

You can kick the people-pleasing habit by envisioning and then working toward becoming the highest version of yourself. You do this by looking within and doing the work on yourself. You make the decision to change yourself and let go of trying to change other people or external circumstances outside of your control. The Serenity Prayer says it so beautifully:

"God, grant me the serenity to accept the things I cannot change, courage to change the things I can, and wisdom to know the difference."

I found a journal entry that I had written a few months ago that outlined this process in my own life. I wrote:

Something has shifted recently. It's hard to put my finger on it, but I am calmer and more relaxed. My trigger button doesn't get pressed as often. Either that, or I don't feel the same way I used to when it gets pressed. I feel a deep strength taking over, a resilience, a surrender. My mind doesn't jump to drastic conclusions as quickly. I'm not as reactionary as I once was. Even when I've been slighted or ignored by some of whom I've considered 'my people'. I'm weirdly okay with it. It's not something I'm trying to feel--the okay part. It just is. I guess I've realized that relationships change. People change. And ultimately it has nothing to do with my worth or not being lovable enough. It just is. I relax into myself. Knowing myself. Loving myself. Being proud of myself. That is what I've been searching for this whole time! Trust in myself. Trust in the divine within me. Trust in surrender. Trust in letting go. Trusting that I don't have to have it all figured out. Knowing that I never will. Surrender is the sweetest scent. Letting go is freedom. Silence is peace. And I am home.

A new, transformed you is waiting as well. The new you is standing around the corner waiting for you to merge with yourself, to become yourself. The new you is ready to take on the world, to live fully, to love completely. The new you no longer pleases others in order to feel valuable and loved. The new you has forgiven those who have wronged you and has healed its emotional wounds. The new you knows its boundaries and limits. It knows when to say "no." It knows how to love itself enough to not have to search obsessively for love in others. It knows love that is deep and profound, divine, and ethereal. The new you can't wait for you to become aware of the weight that's holding you down. It can't wait for you to decide and commit to change. It can't wait for you to identify and heal your emotional wounds. It can't wait for you to establish boundaries and love yourself. The new you can't wait for you to come home.

You are way more than the thoughts you have about yourself. You are way more than the negative beliefs you hold. You are effort, and stillness, and power, and light, and dark, and strength, and mercy, and beauty. You are from the divine and you are held. Safe. Always safe.

Step #6:
Envision & Step Into Your Highest Self

Final Thoughts

Final Thoughts

To you, beautiful one, I would say to you that your life is YOURS. It belongs to no one else. Don't let anyone else put their stamp on you. Don't let them brand you with their thoughts, desires, and beliefs.

You get to choose.

You get to figure it out and you get to follow your own dreams.

You get to create and mold and bend and shape your slice of the world.

Say what you mean and mean what you say.

Be authentically you. If you feel like you've become a shell of yourself, you need to shift. Something needs to give or change or move so that you can become fully who you are meant to be.

You are meant to embody strength and courage and beauty and grace and joy and peace and contentment.

You are a gift to yourself and to the world.

Be gentle as you unwrap yourself. But please, unwrap yourself. Don't stay hidden behind fear or doubts or men.

Release all of who you are into this universe.

The present moment is truly all you have.

Stop running from yourself. Sit with the pain and the heartache. It is there to tell you something.

Stop searching for validation from the outside world.

YOU ARE ENOUGH.

Grow and stretch and learn and challenge yourself.

Be proud of yourself.

Be forgiving of yourself.

But most of all LOVE yourself.

Love yourself with that deep assuredness that you are "the one." Comfort your inner child who was wounded and simply wants to be loved. Show her that she/he, indeed, is good enough.

I will join you in this endeavor. And together, you and I will rise up and we will thrive. We will follow our passion and fulfill our purpose. We will grab tightly to each other's hands, and we will rise. Together.

I started off this book stating all the negative thoughts I used to have about myself. Maybe you could relate to those demeaning thoughts, hearing them throughout your life. I want to leave you with some true, empowering thoughts. Instead of believing those lies, believe these truths...

You are beautiful.
You are strong.
You are powerful.
You are love.
You are courageous.
You are purposeful.
You are complete.
You are ENOUGH.

AKNOWLEDGEMENTS

Thank you to Megan Morgan, Angela Barber, and Julia Fretwell for sharing your stories with me. I have a deep respect and admiration for each of you and appreciate your friendship and insight.

Thank you to Chris Bond who graciously helped with the copyediting after meeting me one time at a Writer's Meet Up group! There are angels among us.

Thank you to Carolyn Colleen for coming into my life at the most perfect time. You inspire me with your determination and ability to dream big and make it happen!

Thank you to Nafsheen Luhar for capturing my highest self. Your art is magnificent, and your spirit is wise beyond your years.

Thank you to my friends, Julie Hughes, Liz Coleman, Darcie Weinberg, Deborah Burt, Wanda Appel, and Janae Terry, for navigating our friendship beautifully and allowing me to be me.

Thank you to my mom, Rachel Burt, for your soft heart and willingness to grow.

Thank you to my sleepover partner, Louis Young, for being gracious with the many boundaries I've set with you, my practicing saying "no" on you, and my ever-evolving process of kicking the people-pleasing habit. You have and continue to be my biggest supporter.

ABOUT THE AUTHOR
JANICE ANGELA BURT

Janice Angela Burt is a court-certified Spanish interpreter, voiceover artist, author, actress, yoga instructor and inspirational speaker. She loves personal development and the evolution of self. She is a seeker, an empath, and a lover of peace. She has two children, Samuel and Ella. She adores them and hopes they learn to speak their truth with love as they navigate their own lives. You can learn more about her at www.janiceburt.com, send her a note to janice@spanishjanice.com, or follow her YouTube channel at Janice Burt, aka Spanish Janice. You can also view her TEDx talk, People Pleasing: An Addiction in Disguise.

References and Resources

Preface
8 "In trying to please all, he pleased none.": Aesop, In L. Harris (Ed.), Aesop's Fables, (Oxford University Press, 2003).

Step 1
7 "Awareness is like the sun": Thích Nhất Hạnh, AZQuotes.com. Wind and Fly LTD, 2022. 09 February 2022. https://www.azquotes.com/quote/479595.

15 "Although most people believe they are self-aware": Dr. Tasha Eurich, "Increase Your Self Awareness with One Simple Fix." (TEDxMileHigh, 3:10), Tasha Eurich, The Eurich Group, November 2017, www.tashaeurich.com/speaking, March 2022.

17 "A people pleaser is someone": Vanessa Van Edwards, "11 Expert Tips to Stop Being a People Pleaser and Start Doing." Science of People, Elite CafeMedia, (n.d.), scienceofpeople.com/people-pleaser.

23 "If we don't spend time with our pain": John Roedel, Facebook posted poem, November 30, 2020, "My love, / take your time / to heal", facebook.com/johnbigjohn/posts/10164128259240276.

27 "Change happens when the pain": Tony Robbins, as quoted on Good Reads, (Good Reads Inc., 2022), https://www.goodreads.com.

References and Resources

Step 1

39 "A traumatic event can be": "Understanding Emotional Trauma", JED, Jed Foundation, (n.d.), https://jedfoundation.org/resource/understanding-emotional trauma/

47 "You can't heal what you never reveal": Jay-Z, "Kill Jay Z," recorded by Jay-Z on the album 4:44 (Hollywood, CA: Roe Nation, 2017).

48 "her anger sapped her strength and energy" Scarlett Lewis, "Scarlett Lewis," The Forgiveness Project, 2022, https://www.theforgivenessproject.com/stories-library/scarlett-lewis/.

49 "he describes paying thousands of dollars": Vishen Lakhiam, The Code of the Extraordinary Mind (New York: Rodale Books, 2019) p. 144.

50 "The five stages of grief": Elisabeth Kubler-Ross, On Death and Dying, (Macmillan Publishing Co., June 9, 1997).

52 "Character cannot be developed": Helen Keller, "The Open Door," (Garden City, N.Y.: Doubleday, 1957).

Step 3

55 "a beggar woman": Eckhart Tolle, "The Parable of the Beggar: The Treasure You Seek is Within You," *The Power of Now: A Guide to Spiritual Enlightenment.* (New World Library, August 19, 2004).

References and Resources

Step 3, continued

47 "I live in a world of movement.":Janice Burt, "I Live in a World of Movement," 2016. Unpublished poem.

57 "Janice - I have had so many 'revelations'": Julia Fretwell, Facebook Messenger text message sent to Janice Burt, January 9, 2022.

60 "Loving yourself isn't vanity; it's sanity.": Andre Gide, author of The Immoralist and other works, circa 1902.

69 "Can jealousy sit in your bones?": Janice Burt, "Can Jealousy Sit in Your Bones?" 2014. Unpublished poem.

70 "Sometimes your soulmate is yourself": r.h. Sin, as quoted on Quotespedia, https://www.quotespedia.org/, accessed April 17, 2021.

Step 4

77 "Pornography is a dealbreaker for me.":Janice Burt, letter written to boyfriend, February 2014, unpublished.

73 "some family secrets": Janice Burt, Bits and Pieces of a Broken Heart, (IngramSpark, 2013).

84 "Surround yourself with people who": Warren Buffet, as quoted on Twitter, "Inspirational Quotes" @Seffsaid, August 12, 2021, https://twitter.com/SeffSaid/status/1426009864019472384.

References and Resources

Step 5

94 "There is a huge cost to your soul": Dr. Anne Brown, Backbone Power: The Science of Saying No, (CreateSpace, June 1, 2012).

92 "You have brains in your head": Dr. Suess, Oh, The Places You'll Go, (Random House Books for Young Readers, January 22, 1990).

94 "Sphere of Choice": Epictetus, The Discourses, 108 AD.

97 "I've missed more than 9,000 shots": Michael Jordan, "Failure" -A Nike TV commercial, 1997.

98 "The size of the goal": Diane Rolston, blog post on Diane Rolston : Clarity, Confidence, Action, www.dianerolston.com/blog, (August 15, 2017).

101 "Decisions without actions are pointless": John Boyd, c. 1950, as cited in "Do You OODA?" Smarter Data: Be Relevant, (Smarter Data, 2014), https://www.smarterdatascience.com/?page_id=l3793#.

102 "All great changes": Deepak Chopra, AZQuotes.com. Wind and Fly LTD, 2022. 08 February 2022. https://www.azquotes.com/quote/521365.

References and Resources

Step 6

104 "If you don't know where you're going": Yogi Berra AZQuotes.com. Wind and Fly LTD, 2022. 08 February 2022. https://www.azquotes.com/author/1321-Yogi_Berra

104 "The only thing worse...": Helen Keller, AZQuotes.com. Wind and Fly LTD, 2022. 08 February 2022. https://www.azquotes.com/author/7843-Helen_Keller

104 "A man without a vision...": Bishop Lalachan Abraham, https://www.speakingtree.in/blog/a-man-without-a-vision-is-a man-without-a-future, June 27, 2013.

104 "The vision must be followed by": Vance Havner, AZQuotes.com. Wind and Fly LTD, 2022. 08 February 2022. https://www.azquotes.com/quote/1184790.

109 Visualization story: Jim Carrey, The Oprah Winfrey Show, February 17, 1997, https://www.youtube.com/watch?v=nPUSbjzLZX0&t=21s.

110 "Search your heart": Lao Tzu, https://truevoices.com/tag/lao-tzu/, November 12, 2010.

115 "God, grant me the serenity" Sifton, Elisabeth. The Serenity Prayer: Faith and Politics in Times of Peace and War. New York: Norton, 2003. Print.

www.ingramcontent.com/pod-product-compliance
Lightning Source LLC
Chambersburg PA
CBHW010448010526
44118CB00019B/2516